# But
# I Wouldn't
# Have
# Missed It
# for
# the World!

## THE PLEASURES AND PERILS OF AN
## UNSEASONED TRAVELER
## BY

# Peg Bracken

*Arlington Books London*

*Arlington Books London*

Also by Peg Bracken

*The I Hate to Cook Book*
*The I Hate to Housekeep Book*
*The Instant Etiquette Book*
*The I Still Hate to Cook Book*
*I Didn't Come Here to Argue*

BUT I WOULDN'T HAVE MISSED IT
FOR THE WORLD!

first published 1974 by
Arlington Books (Publishers) Ltd
38 Bury Street, St James's
London, S.W.1.

© 1973 Peg Bracken
ISBN 85140–229–1

Made and printed in Great Britain by
The Garden City Press Ltd
London and Letchworth

For Kolohe
and the Muehs

# CONTENTS

# Contents

# ACKNOWLEDGMENTS

I want especially to thank Julian Muller, a good companion on difficult journeys. I also wish I could thank Mark Twain, without whom there would have been quite a hole in chapter five.

P.B.

# EXPLANATORY NOTE
## ABOUT THE NOTES

People would have more leisure time if it weren't for all the leisure-time activities that use it up. Foremost among these is travel, which consumes more time than nearly anything else does, except writing about it, as I discovered, writing this book. Though it isn't a very big book, writing it took longer than I had expected. I missed the Estimated Time of Arrival by several months.

My main trouble was in combining the practical aspects with some of the others. Because traveling is full of pedestrian or janitorial details, the book is, too. Yet, rereading the nearly finished manuscript, I kept tripping over some of them, like mops and pails left in the middle of the room.

So there was nothing to do but take them out and store them at the back of the book, chapter by chapter, under Notes, all except for the chapters in which if I removed the practical parts there wouldn't have been anything left. I ran into that problem, too.

However, this seemed to make the going smoother, which I would like to do for anyone I can.

*. . . Still ran Kangaroo, Old Man Kangaroo. He ran through the ti-trees; he ran through the mulga; he ran through the long grass; he ran through the Tropics of Capricorn and Cancer; he ran till his hind legs ached; he had to!* —Just So Stories

# PART ONE

✺

# Some
# General Truths
# &
# Assumptions

# 1

## First Chapter

One evening early last spring, when I was occupying the aisle seat of an airplane flying from Mexico City home to San Francisco, a small elderly woman in a powder-blue knit dress boarded the plane at Los Angeles and took the seat beside me, next to the window.

She was a round chipmunk of a lady with hair that was really unusual, not short and blue but long and gray, and done in a snug topknot. Deftly and methodically she settled herself as though she'd done it often before—shoes off, flight slippers on, shoulder bag under the seat, flight bag on the floor, feet on the flight bag.

Then, on second thought, she retrieved the flight bag, opened it, and removed a somewhat flattened cellophane sackful of what looked like popcorn, though it turned out to be small creamy-white flowers.

"My *lei*," she explained, and plumped it a bit before she placed it carefully under the seat ahead where it was visible but safer. "It's made of real flowers," she added. "Pikake, I think. Not one of those plastic things."

"I can see that," I said. *"Aloha,"* I added, just because I happened to think of it.

*"Aloha,"* she said. Then we didn't say anything else for most of the way.

—Which wasn't surprising. I was homeward bound and so was she, as I learned later; and going home, one is usually silent, with a tendency to sulk. The outward-bound fizz is quite gone, replaced by prudence marbled with an uneasy suspicion that your seatmate might turn out to live right around the corner from you, and this is no time to start anything.

The 747 tunneled its heavy, soft, ponderous, slow-seeming way through the deepening dusk up the coast, somewhere between the mountains and the ocean.

Inside the plane it was dusky, too. Only random spots of yellow lamplight warmed the red curtains, rather cozily. Years ago, when airlines started wooing the general public, they thought hot colors might upset the customers, many of whom were clutching hard at their Saint Christopher medals anyway. Accordingly, they decorated with cold grays and aseptic blues enlivened by a dash of clinical bone, so the interiors resembled the laying-out room in a discreet funeral home and probably scared the customers even worse. This plane was a great improvement. Plummy reds, warm purples, even gold tapestry seats.

The reason I was on it was that I had just seen Mexico, briefly and for the first time, on a fast stopover with my husband, who was in the aisle seat across from me (because he likes legroom, too).

And the reason we had gone there was twofold. First, like having dessert when it comes on the dinner, because a stopover in Mexico City on any NY-to-SF ticket costs only a few dollars more than a direct flight back home, or was supposed to. We realized a couple of hundred dollars later that this didn't include hotels, tequila, and other essentials, but the principle was still appealing.

Second, I was planning to write a book, a book touching on certain aspects of travel. Though I've traveled only a moderate number of miles, I've done an immoderate amount of thinking about them, which should count for something, it seemed to me. But not knowing which places or aspects to include, I felt as the teacher must have when she asked a small Mexican boy how to go about sculpting a donkey and he replied confidently, "It's easy—just take a great big rock and chip away everything that doesn't look like a donkey." I was traveling to postpone chipping.

We'd had a fine fast blur of a time in Mexico, which so obligingly feels like a foreign country the minute you cross the border, and it semed to me that we had seen many things. In Mexico City, we had done the good tourist sights, like the dubious wonders of Xochimilco and Sanborn's Drugstore. We'd seen the splendid anthropology place, too, and the university and the Avenida de los Mysterios, where the Stations of the Cross extend for a good three miles, certainly a grand immortal distance to travel on the knees.

In one of the more unspellable towns, we had been impressed by the baboon-bottom colors of the hot painted-stucco main street, and by the ineluctable authority of the baby-faced torpedo peppers. And we'd found an over abundance of guitar players and serapes and straw baskets and huarachis and Mexican kids on Japanese motorbikes, the new Kamikazes.

Back again in Mexico City the night before we started home, we rather wished we'd left the night before that. Tired anyway after New York, we'd passed our absorption point by several kilometers. Then, in the neon-loud dusk as we tried to ford the torrent of traffic on the Paseo de la Reforma, we saw a bumper sticker, HAVE A NICE FOREVER, and not wanting to embark on ours immediately, retreated to the nearest revolving bar for another marguerita. As we listened to the loud sad mariachi music, I felt a familiar end-of-the-trip suspicion that travel expects too much of me, or that I expect too much of it, one way or the other.

And here we were now, about a hundred horizontal miles and thirty-three thousand vertical feet from home.

It was nearly stack-up time when they turned up the top lights again. Then the plane's stereo system came on, full volume, with some lively piano and the same unerring feel for the wrong country you find all over—"Tennessee Waltz" in Mexico City, the "Third Man Theme" in Nakorn Pathom, and this one, wanting to know how things were in Glocca Morra. It was a good question, though the answer was, probably, Terrible. Nothing but bricks and bombs, the last time I'd looked.

My seatmate was nudging me, in a tentative fashion.

"Big fella box you fight him teeth he cry," she said, her round cheeks trembling with the effort not to laugh.

*"What?"* I said.

She repeated it, then explained. Pidgin English for "piano," she said. Polynesian. Someone had taught her that on Waikiki.

I asked her to say it again so I could write it down. Big fella box . . . And then we talked a bit. She told me she'd been away for a monthlong tour of India, Thailand, Hong Kong, Japan, Malaysia, Hawaii, and some other places I can't remember, and I'm not sure that she could, but nine countries in all.

It was a tour, twenty-six people, and really nice, she said. But she was anxious to get back home now, wishing we'd hurry up and land, because she still had to take a bus all the way to Napa, where she and her husband lived. It would be midnight at the very least by the time she reached her own front door.

"Perhaps he'll meet you at the airport," I suggested. I had rather assumed she didn't have a husband, though I wouldn't have asked.

"No, he never does that," she said. "He doesn't like to go anywhere. He likes to stay home."

"But he doesn't mind if you go places?" I asked.

She answered carefully. "Well, he doesn't *like* it," she said, "but on the other hand I wouldn't say he *minds* it. He's quite a gardener now he's retired, and he built himself a little greenhouse. He raises things, like wild delphiniums." She paused. "Or tries to," she amended. "Anyway, I always go for just thirty days, and before I go I cook him thirty dinners and freeze them. He doesn't seem to like the TV dinners you buy," she said. "So I fix them myself."

"Really?" I said. "What do you fix?"

"Well, he likes a nice meat loaf," she said. "And he always likes pork chops. And short ribs and beef stew . . . and of course cake freezes well, and vegetables, all except potatoes."

I was impressed. I'm afraid I would stay home the rest of my life before I would fix thirty dinners ahead, and I admired her dedication.

"You have quite a wanderlust," I commented. She considered that.

"Well, no, I wouldn't say wanderlust, exactly," she said. The fact was, she belonged to this bridge club, and all the girls had traveled a good deal. One member had even seen the Seven Wonders of the World, she said, except for one wonder, which was in Russia but she couldn't think what it was. (Neither could I, though I thought it was probably a bridge or a dam. Lists of wonders are generally full of bridges and dams.) But anyway, she felt duty-bound to keep up, because the rest of the girls had been nearly every-where.

It was a sound reason, all right, and certainly time-honored. I remembered Johnson's reply when Boswell remarked that there wasn't half a guinea's worth of pleasure in seeing some well-known sight. "But, sir," said the good doctor, "there is half a guinea's worth of inferiority to other people in not having seen it."

I know the feeling; I've had it frequently, that half-guinea's worth of inferiority. But it's hard to avoid, for new in-destinations keep turning up like bright dandelions in the grass. Suddenly everyone is just getting back from there, or heading for there (like a disease you never heard of, and then you meet two cases the next day). And places turn fast now, like cream a day past its prime, so you feel you must hurry; for it is always nice to be able to murmur, Yes, I was there before it got all spoiled and overrun. . . . Although there are compensations, even so. Though the place disap-pointed you, it is still rather fun to talk about how disap-pointed you were.

And there are other good reasons, of course, for going somewhere. Perhaps because you want to avoid something or do something. Or find something or prove something. Or see or hear or taste or buy or learn or teach or forget some-thing (and when you open your suitcase you generally find out that you did). . . . A couple of thousand good reasons for going somewhere, I thought, including the fact that you have the time, the money, and the inclination, or simply the inclination. And you go.

So we circled awhile, like a fat hawk about to drop, then suddenly bored a vertical hole through the cloud layer to find San Francisco down there in the dark, a stretch of dazzle and liquid gleam that could have been Hong Kong or Rio or—for that matter—Pittsburgh. A night plane is a great equalizer.

My seatmate carefully put the packaged *lei* back in her flight bag. That was a nice tangible fringe benefit for her, I thought. And so was—how did it go?—big fella box. At the next bridge-club session she'd be sensational.

And I reflected that she was undoubtedly bringing home some intangible ones, too, as I nearly always do, myself. For one, a warming reassurance that countries are so vigorously, indelibly, endearingly different, and that they will probably stay that way, well into the unforeseeable future. And for another, a fresh realization of what a place the world is. Bristling and ailing but beautiful still, a place to view with alarm and affection, so full of splendid things and remarkable people, with a kind of enduring gumption that never fails to hearten me into taking better care of my own particular patch. Once I get back to it, that is, and catch up with my circadian rhythms and get it all reasonably together again.

So we fastened our seat belts and returned our seats to the full upright position before deplaning, the way the stewardess said to. "Have a happy evening here in San Francisco or whatever your final destination might be," she finished, on a pleasant philosophical note.

Then our captain came on the intercom to thank us for the pleasure of our company (though really we hadn't done much—just sat there, you know, the way you do), and I was sorry we couldn't thank him for the pleasure of his. He had been a congenial companion, all in all, not too conversational but conscientious about pointing out the good sights. It wasn't his fault that they were generally on the other side of the plane and in the dark.

"So keep smiling, the fresh air is good for your gums," he ended as we landed and surged out and up the ramp.

My new friend and I exchanged names and another *aloha* before she trotted purposefully on into the waiting room. And there, standing by the gate was a balding round-stomached man in a blue-checked shirt and a tan coat sweater. Her husband, surely. He had come to meet her, after all. Anyway he hugged her and took her flight bag.

I was glad about that. It is nice to be met when you get back home, especially after nine countries in thirty days, and before that, thirty dinners. She had earned it.

As for my husband and me, we went home and unpacked. And I put my glorious full-color Mexico City travel folders in a good safe place where I never found them again, and four days later I started the book.

One evening early last spring, when I was occupying the aisle seat of an airplane flying from Mexico City . . .

*For myself, indeed, I know now that I have traveled so much because travel has enabled me to arrive at new, unknown places within my own clouded self.*
——LAURENS VAN DER POST

*A trip is what you take when you can't take any more of what you've been taking.*
——ADELINE AINSWORTH

# 2

---

# Newton's Laws of Motion

Gunther Newton, who lives across the street from us, travels a good deal and occasionally delegates me to water the living-room philodendron when he and his wife are away. In return, he has been kind enough to check my manuscript for errors as I've gone along.

One day I happened to see his Laws of Motion, scrawled on the back of an old hotel bill on his desk. He explained to me later that he discovered them up in the attic one night when a suitcase fell on his head, and when he woke up he just wrote them down. At any rate, he has given me permission to include them here.

## I
Deluxe means gyppo.

## II
It is easier to find a traveling companion than to get rid of one.

## III
Any restaurant featuring French cuisine and Ice-cold Grape Slush in the same window can't be trusted.

## IV

A broad-beamed bus driver is a good bus driver.

## V

The longer the cruise, the older the passengers.

## VI

After something is written and published anywhere about a place or a proprietor, they won't be quite the same any more as they were before they were written about.

## VII

He who seeks will probably find . . . something else.

## VIII

(Newton's Law of Universal Gravitation)
By the time you gather together the time and the money for going someplace out of the way, it generally isn't very.

## IX

(Newton's Law of the Ever-level Suitcase)
At the same time an object is lost, used up, given away, thrown out, or otherwise disposed of, another object of equal size and weight rushes in to fill the vacuum.

## X

If something can go right, it just may.

NEWTON'S CATEGORICAL IMPERATIVES:
1. Don't believe the traveler sitting next to you on the bus or in the airport; he wasn't listening either.
2. Don't make funny remarks about the food you

see coming into the dining room; it might be yours.

3. Always carry your own passport.

4. Always have your airline ticket validated at the next stop, no matter who says you don't need to.

5. Always cash your traveler's checks at a bank.

# 3

Never on Monday

*Some matters of timing and time*

The subject of when to take a trip is a matter of frequent discussion in the travel pages: the various merits of spring-time and autumn, of summer and winter, of in-season and off-season. And still other time factors are to be considered. Last week, a friend of mine stopped in before he went to Italy for the first time. He said he had decided he'd better see Florence before it was covered up with mud. "Or before I am," he added, thoughtfully.

Indeed, sooner is generally better than later. In Carmel, California, a pleasant artists' colony gone Fifth Avenue, where the main street gleams with resident Mercedes-Benzes and visiting Cadillacs, one restaurant features a Cappuccino Button Shoes.

"What is that?" I asked the kindly waiter. The only cappuccino I knew about was the San Francisco version— a coffee-or-chocolate-and-milk affair made in an espresso machine and generally heartened with a slug of brandy.

He explained that Cappuccino Button Shoes is the only kind Grandpa can drink: Sanka without the spike, only a little whipped cream. I hoped at the time that Grandpa had had a good run of the other kind, too, when he was up to it.

To get down to specifics, there is no wholly perfect time to get away, any more than there is a wholly perfect time to crack up the car. One aspect of it or another is nearly always awkward, a truth familiar to anyone who ever stared for a long, long minute at a charter-flight schedule.

Flight #192 leaves for London the day before or gets back the day after some happening you are committed to or mired in. Flight #193 would be perfect, but it goes to Berlin.

Or it would be lovely to be in Paris the week of the fifteenth if the auto show weren't. Avoiding auto shows, boat shows, and conventions is harder than hitting them. Or festivals, when the real town disappears under the frosting, and everything closes tight except for the outstretched hands of the cordial natives.

Or one's traveling companion can't make it just then.

Or the place will be too hot at that particular time, or too wet, or too cold, or it will be monsoon season. Or too expensive. Or they just stoned the embassy again.

Or you can't bring yourself to go there now because you can't forget what they did to us. Or what we did to them. Or because of who is in charge now. Like Greece. The mere idea of going there upsets some people. Or Capetown, or Czechoslovakia, or quite a number of other places. (Though, actually, this is hardly logical. Nice people from elsewhere still visit the U.S. in spite of the blacks and the Indians and the Chicanos, and U.S. mainlanders still visit Hawaii in spite of the Hawaiians. The Japanese go look at Pearl Harbor, the Yankees go see Hiroshima. And no one seems to mind about Yugoslavia any more, or Portugal. Or Spain. I know a madly liberal college girl who studied flamenco there all last year.)

It seems to be a matter of how long ago things happened,

twenty years being about the cutoff point. After that, it is impersonal history. So you might as well go, for it will be impersonal history promptly enough.

At any rate, it is a rare and splendid thing when time, money, weather, place, international temper, and traveling companion all dovetail. Usually, at least one square wheel jolts the jaunting cart: you end up going when you can't quite afford it, or shouldn't. Or arriving when the mistral does, and cutting your ears off. Or going to a place you'd as soon not see—which is possible, too, because just as home is sometimes better than anywhere else, anywhere else is occasionally better than home.

I remember trading mountain peaks for slot machines once, because it seemed the only thing to do. We'd packed and said our farewells, had boarded the house key and the dog, all ready to catch the Canadian Pacific for the spectacular train ride across Canada, with a deadline on the East Coast in four days. At midnight the night before, we learned that the railroads were struck. There we were, like the dead atheist in his coffin, all dressed up and no place to go.

So we settled for a few days in Las Vegas, at one of the lavish hotel-motels on the Strip. Ours was just beyond the Chapel of the Bells (complete wedding service, flowers & wedding certificate suitable for framing, all for $30) across the street from the dealers' school next to the big Alka-Seltzer sign. And oh, it was lavish! I can still see our room—done in stunning platinum-blond decor, baby-pink and palest lavender, everything upholstered in unborn linoleum—and the plushy tomb of the lobby with its eleven hundred nonstop slots and the Hot Flashes heating up the Boom-Boom Room. It was an improbable substitute for the snug cocoon of a steam-heated parlor car going clackety-clack over the fir-clad peaks and the snow. And yet it was a cocoon of its kind, too. Sometimes one must get away for a bit, if only down the road.

An important aspect of time is the nitty-gritty one of hours: exactly when things are open or inflexibly closed. This is taken up, in a gingerly way, under Notes, on page 250.

But possibly the main problem with time, and timing, is old-fashioned natural greed. Knowing it is impossible to go everywhere and see everything, still you feel uneasily that you ought to, once you've cut those four thousand filaments that moor you to the home dock. That is usually hard to do, and you want your money's worth. Thus, before you know it, you're caught in the as-long-as-we're-*that*-close compulsion, which eventually causeth the mouth to snaffle, the throat to rattle, and the arches to sag. And causeth the customer to include Madrid for an overnight stand instead of skipping it, which would be better, inasmuch as an overnight stand in Madrid is like *War and Peace* boiled down to a paragraph. And, of course, the real danger here is that the traveler may never bother with Spain again. He can say to himself, After all, I was there, that time, and I didn't think much of it. . . .

*I know it is a shame that I had never seen the noble twin cities of St. Paul and Minneapolis, but how much greater a disgrace that I still haven't, although I went through them.* —JOHN STEINBECK

Worst of all, greed can lead to going nowhere, because some people think, Two weeks aren't enough to see anything, it would be only a waste of money. Let's wait till we can take a month.

But two weeks in the hand are better than two months in the unpredictable future. Moreover, two weeks in a strange place equal six in a familiar one, because of a certain density of experience. Good or awful, it will seem longer. Two weeks might be just right.

This brings up the matter of travel tolerance: quite apart from how much can you take time for, how much can you hold? Like gin or plum pudding, travel is filling. With many people, a little goes a long way. But because they don't know their capacity, they are often surprised when the intensity pales out to a guilty ennui, or crescendos to a pain like a bad sore toe.

Last fall, in Marseille's American Express office, I watched a travel-worn American couple try to reserve a Paris hotel room through a little Napoleon who clearly didn't care if they slept or died. At one point, the lady turned to me with a heartfelt cry. "Oh, I only wish we were *home!*" she said. I could see that their eyes had been bigger than their stomach for journeying; they'd bitten off more than they could do. The trip had hit the fan, but they were locked into it for ten more days.

*Allons, enfants!* To Paris! To Brussels, and Bruges, and jolly old Heidelberg! And still to come was the dead-heading home, culture-shocked, jet-lagged, heavy with that special malaise that can descend like Sunday morning to envelop the returning traveler as he waits in the U.S. customs line with the rest of the sorefooted camels. There is, to be sure, a heartening sense of brotherhood there, a certain comfort in being no longer a *turista* or an *Américain* or a *gaijin* or an *extranjero,* but once again a citizen, in cool command of his own country, or anyway about to be, if he makes it through customs. Even so, the customs line is a long, long hour, which surely ranks high among the more

disconcerting varieties of human experience, right up there
with the divorce and the proctoscopy.

Personally, I find myself on a medium tether. Toward the
middle of the fourth week, the trip becomes an exercise in
controlled impatience, and I toss at night, no cool place on
the pillow. By the end of the fifth, my mind is wringing its
hands like Lady Macbeth. *What am I doing here?* I'm
awash with the conviction that people need me back home,
combined with an equally dismaying suspicion that they
don't.

It can be interesting as well as instructive to graph a
journey when it is over. Some few are a gentle escalation to
the roof garden where you live happily ever after . . .

and some are like a roller coaster . . .

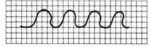

and some are like a ski jump . . .

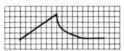

and some rather resemble a trudge across a plowed field, or
a mild cardiac infarction. . . .

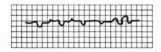

Bearing all these things in mind, then, one shouldn't
worry if the available time seems short. Indeed it is futile
to, because the time boundaries of a trip are so often decided

by great outside forces that aren't amenable to change. Forces like office policy, or money, or some foolish holiday.

One must simply choose from the world's large buffet, bearing in mind that it is hard to be everywhere at once. And nearly always, things balance out. Miss the Brussels sprouts Fiesta at Puddlington-on-Thames, catch sticky-rice-and-mango time in Thailand. I visited Hearst's Castle at San Simeon on the one day of the year they'd let the water out of the pretty Neptune pool (its bottom needed scrubbing, like any other pool bottom). Still, I was in London on the morning the Queen opened Parliament. Very pretty she looked, too, in her glass coach, and I wrote and told her so. (It was rather exciting to start a letter with "May it please Your Majesty"—as one does, you know.) I also enjoyed the courteous reply I eventually received from a lady in waiting.

Win a few, lose a few. One day in Washington, as I was moderately savoring my first cup of the Senate's navy-bean soup, it occurred to me that it was grape-stomping time along the Rhone and I wasn't there.

*Quel dommage,* as we say, we who have been to Berlitz. And it was good enough soup, though lukewarm. The Senate needs a hot tray or a plug-in soup tureen. They can put a man on the moon but they can't keep their soup hot.

Finally, then, to bring us full circle, there is the matter of which day of the week to start out.

Sailors feel strongly about this. Never start on Friday, they say, for on Friday, witches have dominion over the waters.

The first Monday in April is no good, either; that was Cain's birthday and the day he slew his brother. And you can skip the second Monday in August, when Sodom and

Gomorrah were destroyed, as well as the last Monday in December, which is the day Judas hanged himself.

It is hard to see what all this has to do with starting a trip. But as so often happens with some of the old superstitions, closer study finds them rooted in good sense. What the sailors are trying to tell you in their quaint roundabout way is that the day before you leave should be a workable business day, not a Sunday, so you can pick up your traveler's checks and dry cleaning and so on; Tuesday, Wednesday, Thursday—those are all good days. Even Fridays would be all right, except for boat trips.

Too, if you're flying, midweek days are usually cheaper.

Still, advice like this is actually about as foolish as those magazine columns that tell you the optimum time for getting married. The optimum time for getting married is when marriage is proposed or suggested by someone you definitely feel like marrying. The optimum time to start on a trip is when all the holes in the dike are temporarily plugged. Then get out as fast as you can before one of them busts loose again, whether it is on a Monday or not.

Also: a good time to leave is some morning very early, preferably before dawn, through the gray hush and into the radiance. (Once more they've pulled it off, and the world is new again, young, fair, and a maiden again.)

This is especially the best time to leave a familiar place like home for the airport, the highway, the dock, with the random yellow lights in dark houses looking sinful and cozy and most of the rest of the townsfolk competently snoring. They haven't a notion that you're headed for far places. But you know. And even the close-by scenery has a good strangeness before sunup. They aren't the same old streets, parks, gas stations. Then, when the sun is up and working at it, you're in newer country.

And the time to come back home is some evening, later on. Never come home in the morning. You're a little weary, and it's heavy work picking up a day. Also, if you left some people back there, they'd probably rather not see you then. Nothing personal, you understand, and they're probably glad you're back. It's just that it can rather mess up their schedule.

# 4

## The Bird That Flies Backward to See Where It's Been

*I don't know what to expect, as I have given up trying to figure out in advance what any foreign place is going to be like until I get there.*

—RICHARD BISSELL

Good travelers generally do considerable in-depth reading about a place before they go there. They often quote the old Spanish proverb about carrying the wealth of the Indies with you if you want to bring any back.*

And it's probably so. The more you know, the more you see, although on the side of efficiency it is equally true that the less you know, the faster you can see it. Somewhere in my notes I encountered the engaging fact that you can knock off a Bangkok palace in ten minutes if you trot.

I am not trying to make a case for ignorance, exactly—only saying that you occasionally find yourself with a good fresh supply of it, on the way to somewhere. Perhaps it is a sudden business trip. Or Aunt Rhodie decides to test her faith, and leaves you some money you know you could have more fun with than your creditors would. Or you're so busy before you go that there is hardly time to think about the place, let alone do any in-depth study.

Or so I often find it. Another thing I've found is that some people are better at in-depth study than others are, and I am

* There is also an old Transylvanian proverb that says if you start off with an empty suitcase, you can bring more things home.

one of the others. Like overheard gossip about someone I don't know, facts about strange countries don't stick in my head until after I've been there, and not always then.

One year, before I'd ever seen France and was planning to go, I read volumes, carefully sorting out Charles the Fat from Charles the Simple and Charles the Bald and all the rest, only to have the trip called on account of war. It was World War II, which had people majoring in another kind of history. Looking into my mind later, I could virtually watch all that good sound background information evaporating like puddles in the driveway.

Accordingly, since then, I've read mainly fiction* instead of books like that before I go anywhere for the first time. You can't be too careful. Also, I avoid the chatty family-travel-type books people keep writing, because they tend to depress me. They're such darned good sports in those books, and they are always so bright. (*"Oh, Dad!" cried our ten-year-old Ellen. "Isn't this the same style of Manueline architecture characterized by a spectacular opulence that so impressed us at Bélèm?"*)

However, the modern, million-word, many-faceted Comprehensive Travel Guide is a far, far cry from the old histories and handbooks. Certainly, among all the things that are better today than they used to be—ladies' figures, law enforcement, sanitation, sidewalks, clothes, furniture, kitchen sinks, permanent waves, public schools, brain surgery, recorded music, Sunday sermons, insane asylums, grass seed; virtually everything but railroad trains and the fortunes in

---

* Suzy Wong is alive and well in Hong Kong, Somerset Maugham still drinks his gin *pahits* on the verandah of the Oriental, Leonardo still paints. Even if she isn't and they don't, and all the visible changes are for the worse, one's own impression of the place will often fade, leaving the novelist's more vivid one behind, which is all to the good. Like so many things that aren't exactly relevant now, it is more fun to have in the head.

fortune cookies and our chances of survival—the up-to-the-minute comprehensive travel guide* towers tall, leaving Baedeker rueful among the ruins and Ruskin playing with his Elgin marbles.

Indeed, the modern CTG is a good shepherd, for it enableth one to lie down in a clean bed, it restoreth one's soul and body in a decent restaurant, it giveth one a bird's-eye view of the country now as well as then, it steereth one toward the pure waters, the right bus, the museum in the hours the museum is open, as well as the nut-brown ale in the hours when the pubs are closed.

In fact, the CTG's main drawback is the sum total of its many virtues. The fatter and more up-to-the-minute it gets, and the harder it tries to forestall each tiny perplexity, the hairier it makes the whole thing look. One on my desk now contains such an exhaustive dissertation on overseas flight schedules and rates that I'd rather swim over than read it. Beating an egg would sound complicated, too, if you included every last single detail.

Happily, though, as most travelers find out, it isn't all that hard. Unless you are smuggling or hijacking, there is hardly a problem that can't be solved by a good travel agent before it ever comes up. Or, en route, by common sense and an extra traveler's check or the American Embassy. As Jack Smith puts it succinctly, "You stay out of trouble in Tijuana the way you stay out of trouble in Los Angeles or Toledo: by not being an ass."

And so the million-word CTG is fine to pack along and keep handy, like a big cookbook in the kitchen, for occasional reference. But you don't want to let it overwhelm you, and you mustn't exactly believe it all, either. For travel is a personal matter, and travel writers are personal people with

* Fodor, Fielding, Frommer, Michelin . . .

their own slants and biases, whether they are writing travel guides or magazine pieces or Sunday-supplement specials or a book like this one.

For one thing, they'll sometimes put the accent in the wrong places. I once read a pretty nine-page piece about Wensleydale that raved over the view and by-passed the cheese. Obviously he was a scenery man, not a cheese man. But to me, cheese is the operative word for Wensleydale, especially if it is accompanied by a Peek Frean biscuit. On the other hand, a story about Parma that stresses the cheese and skips the Correggios wouldn't be quite for me, either.

So often, it is a matter of the writer's making the wrong assumptions about the reader. A travel book I looked into the other day, written by a fellow who looked like Maharishi Yogi, said the best way to see a country is by bus. He spoke with enthusiasm of busing around the Pyrenees, often with pigs and chickens. But I wouldn't care for that. Though I like buses, I'd rather not ride with the livestock. I've worked hard and saved a little bit of each paycheck, so I hope I won't ever have to, and I don't intend to start now if I can help it.

It's all a part of the popular poor-people mystique, which goes: If you don't hang around the poor people, you're not meeting the people. But I don't see why. You're meeting a great many other people. Walking around, trolley-riding, café-sitting, park-sitting, sightseeing, shopping, meeting friends of friends, you rub elbows with all sorts—urban, suburban, or country folk, professors, housewives, maids, all incomes and classes, including some out-of-work royalty if you want to, for it isn't all that hard to do. If you don't hang around the free soup kitchens much at home, you probably wouldn't feel quite easy in foreign ones. Anyway, you generally manage to see plenty of poor people, one way or another.

*Have a standing rule that many natives should never be allowed to go inside your camp at the same time: for it is everywhere a common practice among them to collect quietly in a friendly way, and at a signal to rise* en masse *and overpower their hosts.*

—FRANCIS GALTON

And there is something else: you can't know what touristic tides may have washed over the place since the writer last saw it. Places change now nearly as fast as the big loaded jets shriek off the runways. Though it may be somewhere in the time warp still, the town the travel writer saw can be long gone to the outward eye. (We have a misinformation explosion now, too, never doubt it.)

Nor can you know how jaundiced the writer was, or how jaded. Some will unaccountably by-pass all the accredited sights in favor of their own unaccredited ones. They'll direct you to somewhere high in the mountain fastnesses of a country that was hard to find to begin with, to some tiny village untouched by time because (as it turns out) even time didn't have a ten-foot pole. Or to a perfect gem of a chapel, boîte, gallery, temple, or garden, unknown to everyone except the writer, and it should have remained so.

I believe that a certain innocence must be preserved, despite the glittering folk who speak of the ritual fitting at Ollero's, the mandatory bullfight at Lisbon.

"Paris has come to seem like an airport itself; everybody is just passing through," reports one of the nervous Beautiful People, which is piffle, for it hasn't and they aren't. Or, "We just did the usual," a woman said, apologetically. "Gstaad, Portofino, Sardinia . . ."

But she needn't have apologized to me. I suppose the astronauts talk that way, one to another. "Just the usual, did a few orbits, picked up a little moon dust . . ."

At any rate, I'd rather not have the five-star wonders of this world sneezed at by some travel writer too blasé for my own good. There are some splendid clichés around, from the Blue Mosque to Yosemite National Park, including the Empire State Building, none of which I want to be routed around in favor of some woebegone pile of rocks out in the boonies. Not that I expect a travel writer to go on and on about how big the Grand Canyon is. But on the other hand, I don't want him to pretend it isn't there.

And on the other side of the coin, you can't know how bubbly a writer was feeling when he saw something, or who bought the champagne. A benevolent airline celebrating some maiden voyage or a cordial chamber of commerce determined to double the tourism take can make a remarkable difference in the reporting.

Thus, there are frequent surprises both ways. Because of a book or a travel piece, you can set forth wide-eyed to see a place that never was and still isn't. Or go reluctantly, expecting the worst, only to find that it isn't that way at all.

A friend of mine was grievously disappointed to see the garbage piled along the trail to timber line on Fujisan, as well as the thirty thousand people climbing it along with her that Sunday in a patient, dark, never-ending line. She had read what an immense and breath-taking experience it was, but she hadn't expected she'd have to hold her nose. Her husband, a happy travel illiterate, wasn't disappointed at all; simply thought the view was great.

I was similarly disappointed in a small Portuguese town, nameless here for fear of souring it for someone else. A magazine article sang of this little mountain place, its turreted antique charm shimmering ghostlike through a froth of strawberry blossoms. And so it bloomed in my mind, a billowy blossomy torrent of pink whipped cream, though strawberry blossoms aren't pink at all, and I know that. I must have been thinking of shortcake.

So we went, and in strawberry season. And it was pleasant and nearly pink, at that, when rosily viewed through a veil of Mateus rosé, though there wasn't a strawberry in sight, not even on the menu. Mainly it seemed a wise old tourist-oriented town, and bigger than I had imagined.

—Which wasn't unusual. It is my own hang-up that I tend to think small. When a writer writes, "And don't miss the charming village of Upsydaisy. . . ." I visualize the kind of place Red Riding-Hood grew up in, or Pinocchio ran away from. A village.

But to some travel writers, village means a town that doesn't have a subway. Or else whatever they wrote about it brought so many people in that it isn't a village any more. Now the tour buses line up like silver whales outside one of the town's fourteen pubs (*trattorias, tavernas, cafés, gin mills*) waiting to swallow their passengers again after they've had their twenty-minute rest stop and bought some postcards proving beyond a doubt what a delightful village it used to be.

And I think, too, of the pleasant surprises. Had I minded all the dire warnings about Paris—how hateful it is to Americans, how ugly it is becoming—I wouldn't have gone back after a dozen years. But the Paris I remembered was still there, gray-green and shimmering. All along her grave glittering streets and in her secret, fresh, merry little parks, she was beautiful still. Various, beloved, and accepting. Companionable, rowdy, funny, *friendly*.

But perhaps the best rationalization for not cluttering the

*31*

mind with facts—whether they are facts or not—is the way they can take the edge off adventure. *Déjà vu* is crowding out discovery now at a great rate, and yet discovery is still more fun than nearly anything. I often think of the man who recently discovered Rome's Trevi Fountain—just ran across it one morning as he strolled about before breakfast. Rejoining his family, he reported that he'd found this really fascinating old fountain. Really quite nice. Some coins in it, too. Odd!

And I remember my own pleasure in happening upon the country graveyard where Gray wrote his *Elegy*. It was on an autumn afternoon, driving back to London, that I found myself in Stoke Poges, a name that rang a faraway bell, though I didn't know why. Then I came to the small cemetery, shaggy and overgrown, even the recent markers weathered into premature old age by the rough English winters. A Berkshireman was lecturing to a docile straggle of tourists in one corner, which is how I knew it wasn't just any old graveyard.

And so I stood there, murmuring to myself a few lines of the poem. Though I realized presently that it wasn't the *Elegy* I was murmuring, it was *Thanatopsis,* it didn't matter. (I know a girl who asked her husband why they play "My Country, 'Tis of Thee" so often in British theaters, too.) I still very much enjoyed finding that graveyard myself.

You could discover the Taj Mahal by moonlight, if you hadn't seen so many pictures of it, and it would certainly be a splendid moment. I doubt if it makes it any prettier to know that the lady it commemorates was the fat mother of thirteen children.

And so I think it is best to settle on one fat marvel of an up-to-date travel guide that comes closest to one's own wave length in what it emphasizes—then buy it, if possible, in paperback.

Then you can read it briskly once before you go, or en route, checking with a red pencil the things you'd really hate to miss, and with a green pencil the practical pointers you might need to find quickly, like how many mangelwurzels to the American dollar or the name of the regional wine. Then you can annotate the pages at the scene of the action and tear them out, upon moving on, to mail home in clumps. This lightens the luggage and lessens the chance of losing them all—which would be too bad—or of lending the whole book to someone and never seeing it again.

For everyone has his own travel history, and it is important that it be preserved. The matter of how is one that we will touch on, if it works out that way, in the next chapter.

*A long time ago I was in the ancient city of Prague and at the same time Joseph Alsop, the justly famous critic of places and events, was there. He talked to informed people, officials, ambassadors; he read reports, even the fine print and figures, while I in my slipshod manner roved about with actors, gypsies, vagabonds. Joe and I flew home to America in the same plane, and on the way he told me about Prague, and his Prague had no relation to the city I had seen and heard. It just wasn't the same place, and yet each of us was honest, neither one was a liar, both pretty good observers by any standard, and we brought home two cities, two truths.  —JOHN STEINBECK*

# 5

---

# On Bringing Some Home

As I pointed out earlier, or certainly meant to, travel is infectious; there is a lot of it going around. Yet, oddly enough, it is infectious without being really communicable.

Indeed, one's travel life is basically as incommunicable as his sex life is, except for the occasional genius, although one's travel life is—of course—easier to imagine. Or, to put it another way, while you can picture almost everyone in the act of traveling, it is difficult to imagine most people coupling, no matter how many movies you've been to. And still the nongeniuses keep trying to communicate both experiences, the sex majors in the books and magazines, and the travelers on the postcards: "Saw the Ganges yesterday—really something!"

In general, more lying is done about travel than about sex, now that a messy or otherwise interesting sex life is considered good conversational material, at least by your encounter group. But with travel, unless there was some truly traumatic development, like a brain tumor, everyone always had a marvelous trip. No one admits to just uglying it away, pouting or sniffling or picking at his cuticle. And even that kind of a trip doesn't seem so bad once memory has had a chance to pretty it up, as it nearly always does, the way the kindly vines cover a raw stump.

Now, it is an interesting fact: although someone else's travel life is at least remotely imaginable, it is at the same time almost completely forgettable. One's own comings and goings tend to crowd the mind, I suppose, squeezing out other timetables and destinations.

I remember an example of this, some years ago, when my parents were discussing a mutual acquaintance.

"You remember Jim Byrnes," my mother said. "Yes, he went to California," my father said. "No, John, he died," said my mother. "Well, I knew it was someplace nice," my father said.

That is the way these things go. Accordingly, you can ask your friend seven times what his departure date is, and receive the information each time with fresh interest because you invariably forget it. Then, after his return, you ask him once again when he is leaving. (*You mean you already went?*) And then you ask him how he found things in Portugal, when actually he did Peru. But you remembered it began with a *P*. . . .

The only exception to this near-total aphasia is when someone comes back from a place you are familiar with, or vice versa.

I know this well. For years I was the only California resident who hadn't been to Hawaii.*

* Hawaii is one of San Francisco's sunnier suburbs, a cluster of one-hundred and twenty-two Pacific islands, a fact few people know unless they just looked it up in the World Book, as I just did. Only seven are inhabited, and their names are easily confused because they are so full of vowels—Lanai, Kauai, Maui, et cetera. Countless generations of tourists would have been grateful had the islands remained the Sandwich Islands, as Captain Cook christened them. Then the seven could have been individually named Pastrami, Egg Salad, Ham on Rye, and so on, and would have been much easier to tell apart.

"We always stay at the Hokahule," the others would say. "They really put out a good breakfast there. Papayas, sausages, muffins, you name it, all for a buck and a half."

"Yes, I know where that is," someone else would contribute. "Personally, we like the Hulahoke."

"Do you? Say, I think I know some other people who stay at the Hulahoke. Isn't that the one around the corner from the Kealakekua?"

"Well, no, not around the corner exactly. It's farther back, if you follow me. Back from Waikiki, I mean. You know where the Kapiolani is? Well . . ."

Before I had visited Hawaii, I couldn't take part in stimulating conversations like this one or even enjoy them very much. But now, having been there, I am able to toss in a few sparklers, myself. "Well, we usually stay at the Princess Papule," I say. "It's awfully nice there, and not too expensive. . . ."

However, with the exception of comparing notes on mutually familiar ground, the first meeting with friends goes along about the same, whether they've been away or you have.

"*How* was the trip?" they say (or you do).

"Wonderful!" you say (or they do). And the next line is, "I want to hear all about it!"

But, of course, no one means now. Everyone means next February thirty-first. Who, actually, can stand hearing the details of someone else's travels? Or even the four-star peak experiences. If any. Imagine listening to Melvin for more than thirty seconds on the Pyramids, or undergoing any of Mabel's sensitive reactions to the Uffizi! Imagine their holding still for yours!

What is lacking for the listener, besides an exit, is immediacy—the shining Look-Ma or If-my-friends-could-see-me-now ingredient that is so abundantly there for the traveler (and no matter how experienced and well worn he is, it is still there in some measurable measure). *It was me! Me living with the gypsies, eating with the Hunzas, getting to know The People! Me plunging around the Métro, climbing Cortina! Me who jumped over the county line or the state border, leapt the surly bonds of earth, over the tall mountains and an ocean, too, to inhabit a far and magic place.* At least momentarily.

And so you head one another off at the pass.

"The weather couldn't have been better. How was it back here?" And perhaps you tell a frail anecdote or two. Then, presently, you notice that the whole trip has shaken itself down to a few incidents you're fairly tired of, but out they predictably come, like burps out of a baby when it's patted right. And if you're not careful, you find all those countries and castles and cathedrals and cafés running together in your mind like raindrops down a windowpane, and any hotel is only another packet of matches.

Thus, as I have said, one's travels are basically incommunicable, as well as a great bore to other people if they are communicated, though it is surprising how many basically sound writers seem unaware of the fact. To quote from a book I picked up and put down only the other day:

Travel sets you apart from the crowd. . . . Many an elderly widow has taken a first trip abroad, only to come home and be the hit of the party with her adventures in almost missing a boat, or walking into the restroom and finding a man in there. It is the action-people who get up and go.

Away from the elderly widow, I think they mean, if she doesn't shut up.

The sorry truth is, travel doesn't set you apart from the crowd any more, it puts you into it—into the long nervous line at the airport check-in counter, onto the roaring high-way.

Moreover, travel never made a bore interesting; it only makes for a well-traveled bore, in the same way coffee makes for a wide-awake drunk. In fact, the more a bore travels, the worse he gets. The only advantage in it for his friends and family is that he isn't home as much. At least there's that.

And so it becomes apparent that travel is a personal thing, with rewards that are mainly personal, too, being so largely the things you remember. Like living in general, it is fairly expensive if you don't remember any of it or bring some-thing back that prods you into remembering. But it is quite a bargain if you do. And so, inasmuch as the colander of the brain usually has more holes than floor, it is important to nail things down.

For many years, people who went on far journeys had an awkward time of it if they wanted to keep a record of what they saw and did. It was necessary to carry along a black box, called a "camera," with dozens of film cartridges. They also had to worry about rain, heat, cold, flashbulbs, bat-teries, light meters, and so on. Also, if it was a good picture, no one would believe they took it, because beautiful slides and prints were for sale all over. And so they had to put Lucile in the picture, which didn't necessarily improve the picture. (That's Lucile in the red coat.)

At the same time, cameras were growing so smart that all by themselves they did everything the photographers used to do, including cut people's feet off. The runaway best seller one Christmas was the camera subsequently adopted by the government for use in IQ tests for chimpanzees. If the chimp couldn't load it in three seconds and get six pictures out of the first roll good enough for the Sunday Pictorial, he wasn't allowed to breed.

Then, one day, an archaeologist made an astonishing discovery. Digging in the ruins of an old primary school, built before green blackboards, he unearthed a small, ingeniously shaped instrument: a slender piece of lead snugly encased in a wooden cylinder, with a rubber eraser on one end, the other end sharpened to a point, and called, as the archaeologist further found, a "pencil" (pronounced *pen*sil). Shortly thereafter, the archaeologist took a couple of these and a blank notebook, along with his wife, Mary Ann, on a busy twenty-two-day nineteen-country tour of the Middle East, and he made further interesting discoveries.

For instance, he found he could make notes in the dark of the moon or the downpouring rain; it didn't matter. (And they could be stupid notes, if God so willed, for no one else need ever know.)

And he found he could make notes about things that weren't photogenic, like smells and feelings and tastes.

And he found he didn't have to pay the picturesque natives if he made notes about them; whereas, in his snapshot-shooting days, he had early learned that they would probably knock him down if he didn't.

And he found he didn't need to worry about his notebook getting light-struck or X-rayed, or worry about getting a lucky shot around the fat lady. Or getting still another shot of another photographer to add to his collection of pictures of people taking pictures.

And he also discovered that he had to buy a camera, after all, and in a strange language, too, because Mary Ann said she had to bring back some snapshots to show the girls, for God's sake. She said that the line in his notebook reading "Mary Ann looked real nice standing outside our picturesque hotel" left something to be desired.

Actually, he was rather relieved; he had found that there were some things he couldn't describe worth a hoot. But he learned that a judicious combination of the two worked out just fine.

I don't mean to imply that the path of the traveling journal-keeper runs entirely smooth. In this, as in anything, there are pitfalls, one of which Mark Twain paints with poignant strokes in *The Innocents Abroad*. Strolling one day on deck, he came across a young man, one of his fellow passengers, busily writing in his journal.

" 'What do you find to put in it, Jack?' " asked Clemens.

" 'Oh, everything. Latitude and longitude, noon every day; and how many miles we made last twenty-four hours; and all the domino games I beat, and horse billiards; and whales and sharks and porpoises; and the text of the sermon Sundays (because that'll tell at home, you know); and the ships we saluted and what nation they were; and which way the wind was, and whether there was a heavy sea, and what sail we carried, though we don't ever carry *any*, principally, going against a head wind always—wonder what is the reason of that?—and how many lies Moult has told—oh, everything! I've got everything down. My father told me to keep that journal. Father wouldn't take a thousand dollars for it when I get it done.'

" 'No, Jack; it will be worth more than a thousand dollars —when you get it done.'

" 'Well, I about half think so, myself. It ain't no slouch of a journal.' "

A few weeks later, Mark Twain encountered him again, in port. After they'd chatted a bit, he said, " 'Now I'll go and stroll around the café awhile, Jack, and give you a chance to write up your journal, old fellow.'

"His countenance lost its fire. He said:

" 'Well, no, you needn't mind. I think I won't run that

journal anymore. It is awful tedious. Do you know—I reckon I'm as much as four thousand pages behindhand. I haven't got any France in it at all. First I thought I'd leave France out and start fresh. But that wouldn't do, *would* it? The governor would say, "Hello, here—didn't see anything in France?" *That* cat wouldn't fight, you know. First I thought I'd copy France out of the guidebook, like old Badger in the forrard cabin, who's writing a book, but there's more than three hundred pages of it. Oh, *I* don't think a journal's any use—do you? They're only a bother, *ain't* they?'

" 'Yes, a journal that is incomplete isn't of much use, but a journal properly kept is worth a thousand dollars—when you've got it done.'

" 'A thousand!—well, I should think so. *I* wouldn't finish it for a million.' "

Well, certainly, anyone who ever pushed a diary down the drain knows exactly how Jack felt. But to my mind, Mark Twain didn't give him the proper encouragement.

The fact is, Jack was suffering from perfectionist's wrongthink. After all, what's France? Your resolute journal-keeper can drop out whole continents and limp back into the ring, punchy but still game.

The thing to remember is that Something is better than Nothing. Therefore, never worry about skipping large chunks. The best journals are patchy, and the worst read like a combination airline timetable and travel agent's tour prospectus: "Wed. Pick up at hotel. Visit treasure-packed Louvre, hist. Nap. Tomb, beaut. Ile St. Louis. FREE drink at famous Café de la Paix . . ."

Another thing to be sure of is to write clearly, using a nonblurring lead pencil or a waterproof ballpoint; otherwise the entire record will rather resemble the Dead Sea Scrolls by the time you get it home.

*It is very important that what is written should be intelligible to a stranger after a long lapse of time. A traveler may die, and his incompleted work perish with him; or he may return, and years will pass by, and suddenly some observations he had made will be called into question.* —FRANCIS GALTON

A discovery of my own is that a number of things can be retrieved even though you didn't take a single note. I learned this once after two weeks around Ireland, when I hadn't jotted down a thing, I don't remember why. But I do remember starting the long over-the-pole flight home with an awareness that I had nothing but a headful of Irish porridge for my pains.

And so I used the alphabet, like a hatrack to hang things on—A for so-and-so, B for. . . . Well, for example, it turned out B was for Ballylee and for Bells and for Butter.

Ballylee meant the poem by Yeats that is carved on the stone at Thoor Ballylee, where he lived, one summer, in the west of Ireland. Remembering it had me remembering around it.

We followed a good-natured Irish bus down the main road that afternoon, just long enough to figure out the placard on its broad bounding rear (TO READ THIS SIGN HOLD BUS UPSIDE DOWN, it said), before we turned off down the quiet green gone-to-wilderness road where the tower stood.

It was more path than road, and there were bees in the raggedy hedge, and old pagan hills standing about, and I remember a family of quail that crossed the road in front of the car as we screeched to a stop. Mother quail are forever taking their children walking in impossible places. It's no wonder Pa always brings up the rear with a worried look. And so it was with this one-bird population explosion, one good Irish mother leading her fifteen babies the size of silver dollars across the road.

I suppose they lived in the tower or behind it. They were heading that way as I copied the poem, in the fading light of the day, on the back of a sales receipt, to recopy eventually on the plane:

> I, the poet, William Yeats
> With old millboards and sea-green slates
> And smithy work from the Gort forge
> Restored this tower for my wife George;
> And may these characters remain
> When all is ruin once again.

I liked the good muscular assurance there. Not *a* poet. *The* poet.

Then, B for Bells meant the Bells of Shandon, in Cork, which I remember now as the town with the permanent flinch. Anyone with the wind and the inclination can climb to the belfry and ring the great bells; for the octave of bell ropes in the big church there is somehow channeled into a keyboard, the notes cued to numbers, so that he who counts may play. The songbook on the keyboard lay open at the "Londonderry Air," though London was heavily crossed out. (This was before the present crossness, but there is always a crossness.)

So I played the "Derry Air" till the town clanged, the big bell-sounds billowing, including the last note when I hit the wrong number, for a great sour klinker. It simply hung there as I crept back down the stairs, and I believe it must be hanging there still, a small funky blue cloud in the amethyst air of the Emerald Isle.

As for Butter, this meant that it comes, dependably, in one of three ways to the Irish dinner table, whether it is a crystal-and-linen dinner table, bare wood, or oilcloth with plates thick as pancakes. Butter came in a scallop, a squiggle, or in a corrugated log, but never in a plain pedestrian slice. You can pick up a lot of useless information if you'll keep your eyes open.

For making notes, some travelers prefer a tape recorder. Even when they are too weak to hold a pencil, they can still talk. Too, they can send the tapes back home to be typed. And some people feel easier talking than writing, though to me it isn't the perfect solution, mainly because of all the places it can't be used—the theaters, the chapels, the 2,000-decibel night clubs, the bedrooms where someone is asleep. Too, you know when a pencil is broken, but not so, necessarily, with a tape recorder. I once confided a fat lot of things to one that wasn't listening, which rather put me off.

Whatever the system, it is important to be selective, of course, in the notes one makes. It seems a great waste to include what is in the guidebook, even though it comes to you secondhand via the guide. Or to jot down anything that doesn't especially interest you. I own to a readily quenchable thirst for details about civic centers and linear measurements of transepts and chancels, though many people have quite a capacity, and they put these things down in copious detail. Which is fine, of course. I mean only that a note should be of some special importance to the notemaker, so that it brings with it a chunk of experience, the way some of the cookie part clings to the chocolate bit in a tollhouse cookie.

I tend toward the feels and smells and tastes and sounds, myself. So I make a note about the teetery nubbly feel to the stocking feet of the bamboo poles of a Japanese moon-viewing platform, and the plump satin of the tatami. Or the feel under the head of the bed pillows, like sacks of flour, in provincial hotels. Or the new-old smells of Rome on a spring morning, lightly spiked with garlic and softened with fresh bread.

Or the early-morning sounds, the siren's sour whine, slithering around the blocks and down the alleys in New York. Or the Mexican audio, an alarum of roosters, a riot of dogs, a resonance of bells. Or the Lisbon doves, mourning early with a tremulous *oooohhhh,* sometimes with only strength for a pained *mmmmmm,* behind the clip-clop of the turnip wagon on the cut-stone street, and the whine-clankity-clank-wheeze of a Portuguese trolley. Or the wild night rain in Brittany pelting hard enough to make immediate applesauce of all the good Breton apples.

Something else I find hard to leave unrecorded is the word. Perhaps it was the old Burma Shave signs along the highways that conditioned me as a child, for they were among the high points of the early traveling I did in the back seat of the family car. I still remember the pleasure of seeing one coming at us, one sign at a time:

SAID JULIET
   TO ROMEO
      "IF YOU WON'T SHAVE,
        GO HOMEO!"
         *Burma Shave*

I remember, too, the mental stimulation of reading the signs on the other side of the road, necessarily backwards, craning around to catch them out of the car's rear window, then turning the verse right side up again in my head, which kept me pretty well occupied all the way to Paducah.

> *Burma Shave*
>> TO JITTERBUGS
>>> TURN JOLLY GENTS
>>>> THEIR MUGS
>>>>> THAT IRRITATE
>>>>>> SOAPS

But the word, anywhere, done in lipstick or marble, is such an alive thing—evidence of Kilroy, and of that universal pathetic desire, as H. G. Wells put it, "to astonish some strange and remote person by writing something striking, some secret one knew, some strange thought, or even one's name, so that long after one had gone one's way it might strike upon the sight and mind of the reader."

And so I find it. It is easy to understand the motivation behind the *Pedro y Juanita* carved on the big gate post in Guanajuato, and the *Try going* UNDER *pay toilets, they're a rip-off* in the San Francisco airport women's lounge, and the peace symbol anywhere it will fit, and the irascible *Revolution is coming, keep your eye on the rich men's yachts* on the Saint-Tropez sea wall. But it mystified me why Anonymous covered one rest-room wall in Manila with *Nothing goes right when your underwear's tight,* though I was impressed by the truth of it.

I collect the admonitions, too. On a damp hotel floor in Kona: WATCHES BEFORE YOU FALLS DOWN. Outside a temple in Nagoya: FOOT WEARINGS IS FORBIDDEN. In a country town on Kauai: BEWARE OF FALLING LEAVES. (Because a leaf there is so often a fifty-pound palm frond that could knock you cold.)

And in France, the most admonitory nation I ever saw: DÉFENSE DE CRACHER, DÉFENSE DE FUMER, in places where you wouldn't dream of *craching* or *fuming*. (Still, you feel that somebody cares.) And the sheer gusto of the Métro warnings. Not just "Danger, Don't Get Off While the Train Marches," but they elaborate. You'll be killed if you try to, they say, and I'm surprised they don't add decapitated. Left in a big puddle of blood.

And the nuggets on the French pottery, after Pascal and Montaigne, by quite a distance. *Un homme sans femme est un cheval sans bride*. But on the other hand, *Pas de femme, pas de soucis*. And yet again, *Pas de mari, pas d'ennui*.

Oversimplifications like this are always a pleasure, for they make everything crystal clear for an instant before it fogs up again. Like some words of Donald Culross Peattie's I saw framed in some Midwestern library: *If your morals make you dreary, depend upon it, they are wrong*. There it was, the perfect touchstone for future action. But then (I reflected further), what if your morals have you feeling perfectly okay but depress everybody else? What about that? And so the truth oozes away again, into the middle distance. All the same, you can chew on these things for hours, in bus stations and airports.

And then the poignant words. The simple *Passent, souviens-toi* on a memorial in a French village. The plaque on the Unknown Soldier's grave at Westminster Abbey: *They buried him among the kings because he had done good toward God and toward his house*. The appealing sign over the alms box in the chapel at Aix-en-Provence: *For the poor, the sick, the ashamed . . .*

And the Latin inscriptions I can't translate. The only one I ever managed to was over the door of the Tickle Pink Hotel (engagingly named for California's Senator Tickle). *Restabit fortis arare placeto*, it said. Though it wasn't easy, I finally broke it down to "Rest a bit, for 'tis a rare place to"; and indeed it was.

But the others—*Castigate ridendo mores? Cantabit vacuus coram latrone viator?* My high-school Latin deserts me. Yet, I keep them because I like them and they remind me of something. A day or a time or a place, a discovery, a meal, a moment, a man, an era . . .

Recently, I was a guest on a chatty TV panel show, talking with a rabbi and an actress about this and that, mainly about marriage. The question arose, Should a couple ever borrow money, and if so, for what? I said they should borrow money for something that would last, like an operation or a journey, not something that wouldn't, like a refrigerator. They thought I had said it backwards, but I hadn't, for I know that with only a gentle assist, you can keep the intangibles far longer.

## 2

*I love to wander around in a good store—it knocks the spots off a museum.* —RICHARD BISSELL

Not that I've anything against tangibles. Not a bit of it. In fact, the itineraries of most trips I've taken could be deduced with fair accuracy from the tangibles layered like geologic strata in my suitcase. I like to pick things up if they are free or buy them if they are not. Like brother Richard up there, I feel that a good store has definite pluses that a museum doesn't.

In museums I often find it hard to know what to say; after dropping a pearl or two about tonal tension or spatial resonance, I tend to run down. But in stores, this isn't a problem. No matter what language you're in, the honorable *How much is it?* isn't hard to ask, so long as the honorable index finger isn't paralyzed.

I even find stores therapeutic. In Rome, once, with a severe case of Vatican feet, I remember how they became instantly A-O.K. the minute I limped into a boutique at the top of the Spanish Steps. La Mendola was the name of it, with a line of silk-wool jersey prints I still cry a little to think about. Why didn't I hock my passport and buy six more?

I especially enjoy buying things outside the United States, because they're usually not sealed in plastic. Still, anywhere will do. Drop me off in the Arizona desert and I'll come home with a sun-bleached purple bottle purchased from some old prospector who owns a big bottle-sun-bleaching factory back in Brooklyn. And if they're selling 3-D postcards of the Rockettes on the boat cruise around Manhattan, save me six. Or ivory netsuke in Kyoto to hang on an obi, I'll get some. You can't tell when you might end up with an unadorned obi, and it is wise to look ahead.

So one acquires things.

And sometimes it must be done immediately. Staying at a small French hotel, some years ago, I was awed into a state of near-catatonic rigidity by two other guests who regularly dined there—two glorious, sultry, doe-eyed French girls, one with a purely spectacular build, her purple suède pants encasing her beautiful rump snug as the skin on a grape, her palest turquoise man's shirt open yea unto the fifth button.

My waiter whispered that they were Juliette Greco, the singer, and her good friend Annabel. Naturally, when I came to, it was imperative to buy a black velvet foreign-intrigue raincoat immediately to make me feel better.

And the trouble with buying things is, once I get them home, I'm nearly always glad I did. I even wish I'd bought some more. And the next chance I get, I do.

Let us make a distinction here, by the way, between merchandise and souvenirs. Merchandise is something else.

Say you know, before you go, that you badly need an amber necklace, and you're going to Greece or Morocco or some other amber place. The first thing to do is learn how to distinguish amber from things that only look like amber. The second thing is to find out what amber necklaces cost at home. Finally, you check your big comprehensive travel guide for the best place to buy it, whether or not to haggle, and if so, how. Then do it.

This takes forethought and decisive action, and it admits of no X factors, like another bottle of wine at lunch. And other things. Perhaps it isn't absolutely amber, but the clasp is so unusual. Or the shopkeeper's child is so appealing. (Many shopkeepers keep one around, from Rent-a-Baby.) Or the Recommended Shop isn't open, but the one across the cobblestones is.

If you can keep your head when all about you are losing theirs, fine. And yet, the methodical approach lacks serendipity; and it is this latter, serendipitous, chancy sort that concerns us here.

Some are chancier than others—for instance, the *coques d'or* one can find and purchase with singular ease on Mont-Saint-Michel, that somber, medieval high-rise off the Normandy coast.

On the way to it, as he drives over the salt marshes, the tourist is informed by large billboards about the general availability of the Mont's official souvenir, *les coques d'or*. But what are they? Something to wear? Hang up? Throw? It was hard to tell from the pictures, salt-faded, though nonetheless commanding.

"Marvelous as the Merveille!" they said. "Don't miss!" And we vowed we wouldn't, as we plunged over the beach, to the wild meowing of the sea gulls, toward that glowering mountain of sea-girt granite, hoping the tide wouldn't make it before we did. When it does, it is a racing tide, like Man o' War in the stretch. Saint Michel au Peril de la Mer. A forbidding rock to build a church on.

That is part of the marvel, of course, that it's there at all, like the flag on the moon—that the bishop could even imagine such a thing, back in the eighth century, and somehow drag all that granite over the quicksand and the water. Or have a lot of other people drag it. He probably prayed while they dragged, and this went on for several centuries, different bishops, different people, because things were pretty messy in France all that time. When this is the case, a country will often do something impossible just to take its mind off itself.

And so we made it; parked, and walked through a stone archway, up the narrow village street crowded with houses huddled into stone walls, and rocks, ramps, ramparts, helter-skelter rooftops, stone stairways, fountains—fountains with husky brass faucets bolted into the mouths of gargoyles who had formerly only vomited the water, unencumbered by pipes. I always think it would have been better if they had omitted either the plumbing or the sculpture in these cases, because whatever the orifice, water usually tastes fresher out of a plain tap.

But it was a minor matter compared with all the complex, turreted rest of it, and the souvenir explosion—shops, stands, and peddlers enough to make Disneyland's Main Street look like a Kansas prairie. Copper cups, trivets, ashtrays, molds, clocks, pots, skillets, goblets, thermometers, plaques, Quimper cups, trivets, ashtrays, molds—

And *coques d'or,* a welter of *coques d'or,* which, as it developed, were anticlimactic small shell-shaped plastic boxes in a fervid carbuncle-pink and a true bile-green, filled with shell-shaped lavender jelly beans.

---

Well, souvenirs are souvenirs, and have been ever since the first pilgrim came back from the first pilgrimage with the first splinter of the True Cross. (Put all those bits together now and you'd have enough to build a stadium.)

In early days on the Mont, the big seller was a little lead phial full of sand. And when *le père* arrived home from his pilgrimage, I can just hear *la mère's* cross "You mean to tell me you paid out good francs for *that?*"

On the other hand, maybe not. Maybe the neighbors came from miles around to see and marvel. And the lead phial—or my plastic seashell, for that matter—was certainly better than a chunk hacked off the thing itself. It is too bad when travelers, like Steinbeck's big idiot Lenny, love something so much they do it in, like the Virgin's veil at Chartres, which is hardly big enough now for a handkerchief.

I don't show my seashell to anyone—never called the neighbors in. But it might have been worse; it doesn't have a Michel Mouse clock in its middle, and it makes quite a jolly little hairpin box that reminds me, now and again, of staying that night on the Mont.

From the windy parapet we watched the high tide streak in over the rocks to lick the cars in the lot far below but eventually go away hungry. That time. And stood and stared beside the dark confessionals in the vast church, somber and virtually resonant with Gregorian chant down the centuries, where it would be embarrassing to confess to anything less than regicide. But the chapel was homy with old wood and personal hand-crocheted things, shabby in the candlelight, comfortable as Mary's own sitting room.

Staying the night there, we learned that the warming French phrase *"tout confort"* means running water near, though not necessarily near you or running at the moment. The handy w.c. adjoining our cell was locked tight, and so we trudged down and up the two narrow stone flights of stairs. But it was a healthy mortification of the spirit, and we thought the old Benedictines probably had it even harder.

And for dinner we tried the famous Mère Poulard omelet, a splendid froth of eggs whipped forever in big copper bowls, and very nice if you like your omelets runny.

A lower point in my souvenir collection is a miniature blue cork-trimmed fishing net I picked up in Brittany, smaller than a breadbox, bigger than a hairnet, about right for a hamster's hammock. I don't have a hamster right now, but the net is around, somewhere, and I enjoy running across it occasionally, because it reminds me to remember Brittany and some of the things I learned there.

About Chateaubriand, for instance. I had assumed he invented steak, till I learned in Brittany that he was a Saint-Malo writer—the vicomte François René de Chateaubriand. It was his chef who developed the particular method of preparing a fillet of beef, for the future delight of everyone with a dependable expense account.

It is too bad that the writer's name is attached to a cut of meat, in most people's minds, instead of to his work, though perhaps he wouldn't really care. The writers I know are generally pretty hungry, and they enjoy their food. The real shame is that the chef who did the actual inventing doesn't have his name on it.

But so it goes. The Marquis de Béchamel probably wouldn't have been able to find his own kitchen, but he still gets credit for the sauce. (It's actually a Milton S. Hershey bar, too, though I doubt if Mr. Hershey himself would have known exactly where to stick the almonds.)

So never underestimate food. The sandwich immortalized the earl, not the other way around.

Then I brought home some Breton rocks, too, to make a cromlech. In the eerie village of Carnak, containing about as many megaliths as people, I learned that a menhir is a stone, and if you put several together, it is a cromlech. Put a long one on top of that, like a hat, and you have a dolmen, if they don't fall over, and these are a good substitute for cave burial, or so it seemed to the early Bretons. I can't quite visualize it, myself.

And so I think about these things sometimes when I see the rocks on my kitchen window sill (haven't quite got around to making the cromlech yet), where they're holding down a leaf from one of the frenzied wind-racked trees on the road to Saint-Rémy, near Arles, the road Van Gogh traveled to the madhouse.

As I say, I like to get things.

In Macao one day, I sat across the lunch table from a lean, tanned woman named Fitch with a short haircut and a mid-thigh mini. She talked about her way of traveling. She was not a shopper, she said; never bought anything but a practical replacement for something worn out. The only thing she planned to buy in Hong Kong—her next stop—was a replacement Pringle cashmere sweater.

"Where?" I asked. I was going to be in Hong Kong again, myself, and it's always nice to have a new address.

She shriveled me with a glance. And she traveled, she continued, with only one small suitcase, twenty-four inches by eighteen. She had been in twenty-eight countries, she said, which reminded me of my Idaho grandmother, who had collected one hundred twenty-two cream pitchers from different places before she died, although six of them were from her own home town and didn't count, as my grandmother was always the first to point out. She was very honest in her counting. But I had the feeling Mrs. Fitch would have counted Hawaii and even Alaska as separate countries. Some people are like that.

Anyway, she went on to say that although she was a linguistic idiot, she always went around alone. Skipped the stores and shops and tailors and stalls, and spent the entire day riding the buses of Hong Kong, she said, just staying on to the end of the line. . . .

This made me feel abashed and timid, as well as greedy. Hong Kong is a real pig's paradise, and I had felt like the monkey with his fist full of nuts in the narrow-necked nut jar, the one who found he'd have to let most of his nuts go in order to get his paw out again.

But then, no fervent shopper could come empty-handed out of that contagious buzz, electric with snatches of overheard shoptalk, thing talk, tailor talk (. . . *he's even putting in a double lining . . . you should see the Shetlands . . . and the most marvelous silks at a fraction . . . I get my third fitting tomorrow . . . ask him to show you the ivories . . .*), and she (he) eventually finds herself with a load too big to carry home.

Happily, though, the fervent shopper can then go buy a six-dollar suitcase to ship her old stuff home in, while she wears or carries the new, which is where she is one up on the monkey. Which is what I did, reminding myself, meanwhile, that we are all prisoners of our genes. Or, as my friend Susan so often points out, "It's fifty per cent heredity and fifty per cent environment, so it's not my fault," a reflection that I find comforting to keep at hand.

As for Mrs. Fitch's mode of sight-seeing, incidentally, I didn't think too much of it. Admired her spirit, certainly, but thought I probably knew some things about Hong Kong that she didn't, because of our knowledgeable Burmese guide, named Cyril, whose bride was Chinese and whose willingness to impart information was never-ending.

———

That spring, Hong Kong was at a fast, rolling boil, like the feverish, bright harbor, the high-rises high-rising before you could look around again. Refugees from mainland China were swimming their three-mile midnight swim to Hong Kong at the rate of about eighteen hundred a month, to find the great bland poster face of Chairman Mao there in increasingly good supply, as the Red Chinese stores opened to roaring business. It is entirely possible they'll wake up some morning in 1997, when the British lease runs out, to find that it wasn't renewed and they never left China, after all.

But no one seemed to be worrying. On they came, in wet, determined droves, some to squat on rooftops, living on oyster plant and sweet potatoes, the rest going into the big new resettlement beehives. And came the Japanese tourists, formicating* like mad, dark endless lines of them behind a pennant-flourishing leader. And the Western tourists, clutching their cameras and address books—all the special little tailors and restaurants, and the divine little shops . . .

Cyril took us to Aberdeen (Shekpaiwan), where the river people stubbornly live their jolly, walloping, huddled anti-hill lives on the water, while the sterile skyscratchers built for them stand staring, many cubicles empty. The floating population knows that's no way to live; they'd rather float. Who wants Sing Sing after Coney Island? What price twentieth-century amenities? And on beyond, in the New Territories, we saw the women of the strange Hakka tribe, drearily digging in the ditches and the fields.

The Hakka ladies haven't received the liberation message yet. They do the men's work and the women's, too, while the men loll around the teahouses. And they wear Hakka hats, great straw circles fringed all around with black muslin for flicking the flies away, Cyril explained, when they're up to

* A perfectly respectable word that means "moving like ants."

here in filth. They work like dogs and roar like tigers when you take their pictures, unless you tip them handsomely. And if you photograph their hovels, they'll claw your eyes out and you can hardly blame them, for you've frightened away the spirit of the house, and it won't come home again.

Then, driving through the countryside, we saw the big armchair tombs, like tilted bathubs. Cyril explained that these were a rest-and-recreation facility for the ancestors, something for the spirit to sit on when it came up for air. (What would Mrs. Fitch have made of them—picnic benches?)

And Cyril told me solemnly about bone-polishing. He said that it hadn't been written about, anywhere, and if it is in any other book I'd rather not hear about it. Five years after the funeral, the eldest son cleans his father's bones with Chinese wine. (But only Father's. Mother gets to rest hers forever and ever.) After that, it is his privilege and responsibility to repolish them annually, and should he leave the region, he hires a professional bone polisher to do it for him. I doubt if Mrs. Fitch knows that either.

The truth is, roaming solo in very strange country can soon become a mindless enterprise. Signs you can't read, prices you can't translate, buildings whose purpose you can't surmise, foods you can't name or taste on your mind's tongue, so that it is almost like not seeing any of these things at all, I thought, in the long, low, tin-roofed Hong Kong market, where some small baking potatoes turned out to be another breed of mango, next to some broccoli trying to be goldenrod that Cyril said was lovely steamed with oyster sauce, and a hundred other things, from homely dried duck livers to beautiful glazed rooster claws and cerebral tonic pills.

And Cyril explained about the Chinese clothes, virtually unisex, though the man's blouse has pockets on the top, the woman's on the bottom, the man's jacket opens in the middle, the woman's at the side, and the man's trousers have no fly, he said, nor the woman's, either.

Even table manners. Rapping on the table says "thank you" if your mouth is too full to talk, Cyril explained, after doing so. (I thought at the time, Really? A guide could provide some interesting misinformation if he wanted to, as well as some innocent merriment for the natives. Puff your cheeks to say "excuse me," scratch your backside to say "you're welcome." Like some parents I know who taught their infant that puppy-dog meant automobile and kitty-cat meant breakfast, and so on, just to see what would happen. What happened was that they all started talking that way and didn't come unscrambled for years.)

At any rate, the table-rapping was received in the proper spirit by our Chinese waiter, and I filed it away in case I ever get to Peking, though it's probably better etiquette not to fill your mouth so full to start with.

Anyway, nuts to Mrs. Fitch and back to souvenirs, and to the matter of which ones translate. For you can't predict.

In Denmark I bought a delicate line drawing of *Schadenfreude*—the obscure glee one sometimes feels at someone else's misfortune—and it seems to hold up well. It is a universal trait, I suppose, that's at home anywhere. But my Portuguese *sogra* was a practical disappointment. *Sogra* means mother-in-law; it is also the word for the padded ring —like a fat cloth doughnut—worn by the black-clad women on their heads, under the basket of fish or box of bricks they carry there to leave their hands free. Though I didn't plan to haul my bricks that way, I thought a *sogra* would be a good pincushion, as well as a memory of those handsome, tall-walking people. And indeed it does remind me of many things, though it is impervious to pins.

And my Viennese steak knives, whose horn handles are so

thoroughly curved that the knives roll off the plates. Nevertheless, it keeps the guests on their toes, while I think of a uniquely European and beautiful city that I must go see again, someday.

And *leis* don't translate. They look ill at ease on white-skinned people, like tikis on a Federal mantel. But if a *lei* reminds you of a Hawaiian honeymoon, or simply a rosy sunset, you should probably bring it home.

A great deal of souvenir snobbery is going around now, mainly because so many people are. This seems too bad, because what is Out is generally what the country does the best job of making: the Scottish kilt, the Irish sweater, the shrunken head, the evzone doll, the dirty French book, the Tahitian coral jewelry, the Viennese needlepoint, the Mexican serape, the beaded Hong Kong sweater—all those things.

I suppose the real trouble is that they don't necessarily say you've been anywhere besides downtown. It wasn't long ago that a collection of hash pipes meant you'd been to the Orient or at least had a seafaring uncle. But no more. Equally uncommunicative is the ingenuous handcrafted folkware that some huge machine started to turn out in quantity in the late sixties—lumpy brass, macramé, and the massive leather bags that only a camel could carry—most of it looking about the same from Israel to the East Village, including Bellevue, Illinois.

It is true that certain items, at the moment I write, have a certain moderate status, because they are not yet being imported in large quantities: the hair style by Alexandre or his Paris successor, or a dirty Arabian book, or Sei Shōnagon's *Pillow-book,* or an ethnological recording from Chad, or a handsome cotton dress from Thailand, or even Levi's from some unlikely place like Innsbruck or Kowloon. Or a deed to an island, or a Scandinavian maid, or a good speaking knowledge of Bengali.

But inasmuch as thing-dropping is difficult and status items go In and Out like the tides, it is wisest to get only what really pleases you, In or Out, cliché or trendy, but get it, then and there. It's no good saying to yourself, Well, I'll be seeing them all over, so I'll wait till just before I leave. Chances are excellent that there won't be another exactly like that one. So buy it. And if you find an even better one later, get that, too.

Here are six helpful suggestions about souvenirs, not valuable enough to go under Notes at the back of the book, but nonetheless practical.

1.  *Baraka* is a good thing to look for. This is an Arabic word meaning the particular charm adhering to anything, from a cooking pot to a mosque, that has been long used, by either a person or his clan. *Baraka* runs wild in the flea markets, and it makes a lovely memento. You know there isn't another precisely like it, and it is duty-free if you can prove it is over a hundred years old.

2.  It isn't hard to age your own souvenirs for a kind of instant *baraka*. A Taxco antiques dealer told me that to make things look genuinely old, he soaks them in dirty crankcase oil, sets fire to them, douses the fire, dunks them in fuller's earth or ashes, then brushes them off. This doesn't do much for cheese or an oil painting, but it works nicely with wood, and it keeps alive many an antiques dealer who otherwise wouldn't be.

3.  The Connemara marble earrings or the divi-divi dress will seem unique at home, away from the shopfuls in Dublin or Curaçao. Remembering this, you should get one before they have a chance to bore you, ever mindful that the ardent

shopper regrets only what she didn't buy, never what she did.

4.     Shopkeepers are awesomely honest about sending things, it just takes some longer than others to find the string. Though there must be exceptions, I've never found one, after tempting fate in some idiot ways. With any cash purchase, exuberance is good. *What lovely things you have! I'm going to tell all my friends to come here! What is your name, please? I'll tell them to ask for you!* But I don't always think of doing it, or else the shopkeeper speaks only Tagalog. Even so, the purchases arrive.

5.     Some people are natural bargainers and some are not. For those who are not, a possible ploy is wistfulness—the thing is so beautiful, I'm unutterably sad that I can't afford it. Usually the merchant agrees; tough apples. But should he sympathize and knock a peso off the price, the nonbargainer should pay it and run. I pass this advice along only for what it is worth: one peso.

6.     The best place to buy gifts for people at home is the Port of Entry, upon return, if it is New York, Los Angeles, San Francisco, or any other city with an international bazaar or a comprehensive import shop. Or New York's United Nations gift shop, which carries an astounding number of good things. I was especially impressed by their Gee Haw Whimmy Diddles from North Carolina and the excellent collection of Japanese *darumas*. These are the round-bottomed dolls that won't stay down no matter how often they're clobbered, which makes them a good souvenir for the traveler, too.

If one of these cities happens to be home, you can shop there at leisure before you leave. Otherwise it is risky, because itineraries can change. It is hard to explain returning from Yugoslavia with a load of shillelaghs. Therefore, people whose homes are elsewhere find it best to allow another day at the end of the trip. In any case, earmark a traveler's check.

Buying gifts here isn't unethical. What your friends want is an object, which they get, or the knowledge that you thought of them. And you did.

But the traveler must operate from enlightened self-interest. To him, after all, the souvenir is larger than itself, bearing some of the trip within it. Like the note in the notebook, or the snapshot, it helps keep the journey in the active file. For the trouble is not that one doesn't remember, if the memory is called to one's attention. The trouble is that one can forget to remember unless it is.

# 6

## The Best of Everything, So Far

These pages are to fill with your own nominees, some rainy night, so they won't get away. The best:

airline _____

alley _____

avenue _____

bar _____

bartender _____

beach _____

bed _____

bookstore _____

bread _____

breakfast _____

bridge _____

building _____

canapé _____

castle _____

ceremony _____

chapel _____

cheese _____

church _____

city _____

club _____

country _____

country road _____

dessert _____

dinner _____

drink _____

drive _____

encounter _____

flight _____

foul-up _____

fruit _____

gallery _____

golf course _____

guide _____

harbor _____

highway _____

hotel _____

inn _____

inscription _____

island _____

jungle _____

lake _____

library _____

market _____

meal _____

memorial _____

moment _____

motel _____

mountain _____

museum _____

ocean _____

painting _____

performance _____

pool _____

pub _____

restaurant  _____

river  _____

road  _____

room  _____

ruin  _____

seashore  _____

ship  _____

shop  _____

shrine  _____

sound  _____

soup  _____

souvenir  _____

statue  _____

street  _____

theater  _____

tour  _____

town square  _____

tree  _____

valley  _____

view  _____

walk  _____

walled city  _____

wind  _____

wine  _____

wonder  _____

# PART TWO

# Some Areas

# of

# Light

# Turbulence

# 7

## Clam Juice Subject Wish to Explain Thing Is

A book of mine, *The I Hate to Housekeep Book,* was being translated into Japanese, and the translators were apparently having trouble. One morning, a special-delivery letter came from Sachiko Kushira, in Kyoto:

> On page 46 of the book is found the lines,
> "But this is a lot of clam juice. You are still
> ironing; and if ironing makes you come all over
> introspective, . . ."
>
> What is "clam juice"? At first it appeared to be one of usual American idioms found in any dictionary. But I could not find, and I should be very glad if you would tell me the meaning. Does it have any connection with the "clam juice" in your *The I Hate to Cook Book?*

This was quite a question, all in all, for so early in the day. I had to sit down and drink another cup of coffee and think about it.

But I could answer the last part of it straight off: Well, no. This particular brand of clam juice wasn't the kind that comes in cookbooks; and because it was literary, not culinary, I doubted that a literal translation would deliver the real message. Word-for-word translations so seldom do. When they told the big computer to rephrase "Time flies

like an arrow," it thought it was easy and replied, "Time-
flies enjoy eating arrows."

In my Japanese dictionary, clam is *hamaguri,* and juicy
(I couldn't find juice) is *mizuke no aru.* I thought *mizuke
no aru hamaguri* would probably sound about as funny to a
Japanese as a case of blowfish poisoning. Sachiko would certainly have to look farther afield.

Still, I wanted to explain to her why I had chosen clam
juice for that particular sentence; and this was hard, inasmuch as I didn't know quite why, myself. I had to think
back, wishing meanwhile that I were as good at this sort of
thing as the editors are who do the footnotes in textbooks.
They can explain exactly why a writer used the words he did,
often to the writer's surprise when he sees it. Usually, the
writer just used it because it was there. And perhaps he
didn't even like it very much; perhaps he'd have put down
something better if he could have. Sometimes writers can't
be choosers.

This particular kind of clam juice came along in a discussion of the rollicking hemorrhoids-can-be-fun approach to
housework, specifically ironing, which is often found in Advice to Homemakers articles. They tell you (I said) to put
on a fresh housedress, whatever that is, then turn on some
music, sit down happily behind your ironing board, and
have yourself a blast, ironing.

Accordingly, clam juice meant nonsense.

But I didn't want to say nonsense: it was too literal. Or
bosh or twaddle—too British. Or baloney or applesauce,
which stopped being funny, if they ever were, long ago. Or
horsefeathers, which is a spin-off from horse manure, and
you wouldn't want that near the ironing board. Anyway, the
rhythm wasn't right.

So clam juice came along. It didn't have the disadvantages of the others, and in addition it seemed mildly funny. No barn burner, but okay. And why was that? Because of happy as a clam and tight as a clam? Or was it faintly evocative of Mrs. Murphy's chowder and the overalls? I had never assumed that her chowder was a clam chowder, exactly. But, these things perhaps lurk in the subconscious.

Moreover, there is the not-so-simple fact that some words are naturally slightly funny, and some are not. Clam juice is, but orange juice isn't. Brother-in-law is, but brother isn't. And so on.

Clearly, all Sachiko needed was an informal, offbeat Japanese word like this, one that wasn't out of place in a kitchen, one with the proper rhythm and coloration, preferably with a peripherally allusive element touching upon something comical in the national folklore, and one that sounded mildly funny in itself. I wished her well.

And so, answering her letter, I suggested that she find a cheerful synonym for nonsense. I wasn't about to lead her into the rest of that Cloud-Cuckoo-Land and have her weeping into honorable typewriter.

I've wondered since what word she used. *Sushi?* Those are the small vinegared rice balls. Or *sashimi?* That's the raw fish. "That's a lot of *sashimi*" sounds pretty good in English. But it probably wouldn't in Japanese. Anyway, *sashimi* is is fresh, light, delicate, and usually expensive, quite the wrong connotations.

Well, I wish I were able to read her translated version. I trust Sachiko implicitly, and I'll bet it's a howl. I'll have to learn Japanese.

But what do you make of a language that has over a hundred ways of saying the pronoun I? No wonder they simply skip it half the time; they can't make up their minds. What do you make of a language that has the dogs barking *wan-wan* instead of *arf-arf?* And pigs oinking *bu-bu?* What do you make of a language that ends all its words with an *n* or a vowel, so they all sound like boron or cuticura, and writes Chinese but reads Japanese, with two alphabets that aren't alphabets at all but flocks of syllables like silvery bird chatter, and then casually shuffles the whole thing so it's backside to?

Hash, that's what you make of it. The Japanese started giggling centuries ago because it was considered polite; and now they probably couldn't stop giggling if they wanted to, for listening to what the tourists do to the language.

*Could you learn all the words in a Japanese diction-ary, you would not make yourself understood in speaking unless you learned to think like a Japanese —that is to say, to think backwards, to think upside down and inside out.* —LAFCADIO HEARN

In the few short weeks I was in Japan, I learned approximately five things in Japanese—a little better than one a week—and, considering everything, I didn't think that was too bad.

I learned to answer the telephone with the brisk *Moshi-moshi* that means *Say, say!* or *By all means speak up if it so pleases you.* The caller certainly did speak up, pouring a torrent of verbal Japanese noodles all over me, and then confidently awaited my reply. I decided not to do that any more.

The second thing I learned, on a train to Nagoya, was the word for privy—two words, actually, which differ according to one's sex, though the facility itself is often the same for both. Men call it the *"benjo"* and women call it the *"gofujo,"* meaning honorable motion place, which is 100 per cent correct when it is on a fast train over a rocky roadbed. The *gofujo* is a shallow oblong trough flush with the floor; and keeping your balance in medium heels is a neat trick if you can do it, though otherwise it isn't.

I also learned *Koko doko,* which means Where are we? *"Koko doko?"* I would ask my husband when we got lost again among the doves in some misty-gray temple yard. "Search me," he would reply, in one of our many stimulating bilingual exchanges.

Finally, I learned that Ian Fleming didn't know what he was talking about when he said there is no profanity in Japan. Reading *You Only Live Twice,* I had been surprised by that flatfooted pronouncement. It was James Bond's Japanese mentor who said, "No swearing, please. There are no swear-words in the Japanese language, and the usage of bad language does not exist."

Really? I could hardly believe it. Here was a country smaller than Michigan, crammed unto crying with enough people to equal more than half the population of the entire United States, and this country didn't swear? After only two days there, I'd found a good selection of things to cuss about, from the way they kick you onto the trains to the taste of the pickled turnips. Found plenty to love, too. But all the same. Not cuss? Ever? *Mama-san!*

And so I was delighted to have a chance to put the question, one day, to a young Japanese bridegroom on board the boat to Beppu. This was the honeymoon special, and I don't know what I was doing there, though I've an idea what I should have been. Dozens of hand-holding couples were aboard the shabby little ship, the girls in pretty kimonos, the men in their dark beetlelike business suits, all bound for Beppu, the Japanese equivalent of Niagara Falls, over the Inland Sea.

It was in the lounge before lunch that I talked with one of the brand-new husbands, who seemed eager to practice his Engrish. His pretty bride only giggled, when she wasn't picking her teeth—they do a great deal of teeth-picking in Japan, and it's perfectly polite so long as it's done behind one's handkerchief, as she always did.

When I asked Mr. Maeshiro about profanity, Mrs. Maeshiro giggled harder than ever, and I was afraid I'd been terribly gauche, though it turned out that she understood only Japanese, and was giggling because her husband was.

Between giggles, however, he assured me that Ian Fleming had been grossly misinformed. The Japanese, he said, cuss prenty.

"What swearwords do you say?" I asked.

He thought.

"Say *shimatta*," he said, hopefully. "That is—how you say—confound it!"

It seemed to me as good a euphemism as shucks is, for people who don't like four-letter words. But I must have looked disappointed, for he thought some more.

"Say *chi-ku-sho!*" he said, and here his wife giggled so hard I thought she'd fall on her kabuki. "That is—how would you say—Goddamn!" he explained, with gusto. "And *kono-yaro*—bastard," he continued. "Son of a—"

"That's fine, just fine!" I interposed quickly. I could tell that he had some jim-dandies still up his sleeve, and I didn't want his little bride to giggle herself right off the boat. But I wanted to thank him, and it so happened that only that morning I had memorized a lovely Japanese thank you. *Makoto ni go shinsetsu de gozaimas,* meaning In truth, an august, special, lordly amiability is here honorably placed.

Naturally I couldn't remember it, now I needed it, and so I expressed somewhat the same noble sentiment in English. Indeed, I was grateful, and glad to know, too, that my hunch had been correct. The Japanese cuss fruentry, on occasion, even as you and I.

Language is a problem in any language, all right, for someone who speaks only his own. One day I was talking about travel with a great Dane I know—a charming, well-traveled, and knowledgeable citizen of Denmark, fluent in Dutch, French, Italian, German, English, and scrappily acquainted with two more. When I asked him what he considered the difference between a traveler and a tourist, he replied promptly that the difference was in speaking the language.

"Then you learn something of the real country that is behind the façade," he said. "And then you're a traveler. Otherwise you are a tourist." And tourist, as everyone knows, is a dirty word which immediately summons to the American mind a picture of the sweating sport-shirted male, umbilically attached to his camera, and his fat befuddled consort—she's the one in the mink stole and the white shoes.

This is too bad. So often it isn't so. Some of my best friends are tourists, and they don't look like that at all.

However, if my friend's definition is correct, it is apparent that we are all doomed to be tourists most of the time, including my friend, once he gets out of the Common Market. As Henry Dreyfuss has pointed out in his *Symbol Sourcebook,* "there are today some 5,000 languages and dialects in use throughout the world, of which perhaps a hundred may be considered of major importance. In most instances, intercommunication among them ranges from difficult to impossible."

And this, of course, is why travelers depend more and more on signs. The old Tower of Babel would sound like a Quaker think-in compared with the five-thousand-language world we rush about in today. Though few of us know Esperanto or Suma or Interlingua, nearly anyone from anywhere receives an immediate message from the standard symbols for Poison, Falling Rocks, Women's, Men's, Drinking Water, Don't Cross, and a good many others. New symbols keep appearing, too, to swell the more than twenty thousand in the Dreyfuss Symbol Data Bank already.

Perhaps this is the look of the future, and we'll come full circle someday, from the caveman's first pictograph around again to the world citizen's. And then, with that universal language refined and enlarged to cover all areas from commerce to poetry, as the experts say it will be, we can leap the five thousand language fences that hedge us in and finally—they predict—achieve a peaceful world.

It is an engaging field for speculation. And yet I wonder about it, for it seems to me that the more communication we have, the more trouble we are generally in.

Even as individuals. If speaking one language were a guarantee of peace, most marriages and friendships would endure. But they don't, and often because they communicate themselves to death. So many people insist on Talking It Out instead of Shutting Up; and talking it out adds fuel to the fire. In fact, not understanding someone can be a great source of love, comfort, admiration, friendship, and all sorts of other good things. God save us all from being totally understood; for there is more truth than humor in the old line "You really have to know him in order to hate him."

And so with nations. If speaking one language were the answer, the United States would be a tranquil land; for in spite of all our dialects, from Internal Revenue Service talk to Madison Avenue, 99 per cent of us can understand each other. That's just the trouble. As for nations getting along

together, all the multilinguists at the UN haven't been able
to put out the grass fires.

And so I hope the symbol people are right, though I am
afraid they are wrong, and that our salvation lies elsewhere.

Meanwhile, the life of the traveling nonlinguist isn't all
bad, and I don't think the point has been sufficiently stressed.

Granted, you miss some overheard snatches of talk. And
yet, when you come right down to it, how many snatches
overheard in English are really worth overhearing? Precious
few. At one time, certain inventive people were playing a
game in elevators. Getting off, one murmured to the other,
just loud enough to be overheard, "She said to tell you she
left the body on the dumb-waiter" or something equally in-
triguing. But now, with these pixies not around, and I don't
know where they went, pickings are usually slim. "Okay,
you pick up the dry cleaning and I'll get the dog food. . . ."

Arabic is a beautiful-looking language—so stylish, I think
—and once, in Fez, I was maddened with curiosity by a
small discreet placard full of the lovely stuff thumbtacked to
a secret-looking gate on a side street. As I stood puzzling, a
kindly bilingual passer-by stopped and translated. It said,
roughly, "Thank you for coming. We have moved to a new
location to give you even better service." A firm of book-
keepers, I believe.

The only language besides English that I have any acquaintance with is French. For years we have carried on a
flirtation, French and I, but have never quite achieved a
complete and meaningful relationship, as I believe they put
it now. Probably we never will; there'll always be an inter-
ruption, and I'll continue to paddle in the shallows of Comfort French—menu French, hotel French, courtesy French
—never quite making it into the deep end.

Of course I am sorry about this, in a way. French is such an admirable language—so precise an instrument, so lively, so invigorating, and mainly, so logical, though I admit to its maddeningly illogical aspects. I consider it inconsiderate of the French to pronounce their river Lot the way it is spelled, to rhyme with hot, and to say "Aches"-en-Provence instead of Aix, to rhyme with hay, as one would expect. This puts you in the awkward position of speaking right and sounding wrong, to your more ignorant friends. And why do the natives of Laressingle call it "Larry-Single"? Better just not mention those places when you come back home.

But these things can be forgiven because, as every lover of the French tongue knows, everything sounds so much better in it, or on it. And it is here that the French people are surely the losers. With one's native tongue, the meaning hits the mind before the sound does, or at least simultaneously, and the sound goes begging.

For example, it may be true that cellar door is the loveliest word in the English language, as H. L. Mencken remarked, but I must first get the angular, unlovely image of the thing itself out of my head before I can hear the melody. And so with French. Koestler mentions somewhere the pure beauty of *L'usage du cabinet est interdit pendant l'arret du train en gare*—how it melts away like the music of the spheres. But the Frenchman would perceive instantly that he mustn't use the toilet while the train is standing in the station; and the practicality of the message would obscure the harmonics.

And so the language innocent is, in one way, ahead of the game. *Pattes d'oie* sound more charming than crow's feet, as *chair de poule* is daintier than gooseflesh. *Glace, tous parfums* is more appealing than thirty-one flavors, even though the ice cream isn't as good. Driving along the country roads, I like *Passage des Grands Animaux* better than Watch Out for Cows; and to me, *Mardi: jour de repos* has a nearly celestial serenity, which you can't say for Closed Tuesdays.

Then, there is something else: I think the American is one up on many a foreigner where a particular language is concerned, because he generally knows he can't speak it, and doesn't pretend to except under stress. But people in other countries have apparently read so much of their own tourist bureaus' publicity ("virtually everyone in Lower Graustark speaks English") that they believe this is what they are doing.

After much thought, I finally figured out that the Japanese *Preeshot oteru?* means Please, what hotel are you in? The Frenchman's *shuck-LATT* bears the same relationship to chocolate that an earnest Yankee's *caFAY-o-LATE* does to coffee. I remember a pleasant Frenchman in Roquefort-sur-Soulzon, the home of the lovely cheese. Over an *apéritif,* after we'd toured the cheese place, the talk turned to art; and he mentioned with pride a painter friend of his who, he said, had exposed himself in all the major capitals of Europe.

So perhaps the Instant Language handbooks would do better to teach the kind of pidgin that the host country speaks to tourists, and forget about trying to teach the country's own tongue. Such a handbook—English as the natives really talk it—could be handy in many countries. I can visualize Frenglish, Spanglish, Itanglish, Germanglish, Japanglish, Chinglish, and—oh, definitely—Thainglish. For in Thailand, where the people move like dancers and the dancers move like angels, English is transmuted into something rich and strange and bearing virtually no resemblance to the original.

Thais have real trouble learning it in the first place, according to a teacher I met there. And, often, the Thai learns his English from a Thai who learned his English from a Thai who . . . at which point the situation is clouded beyond repair.

My own theory is that the Thais use up all the linguistic talents they have in learning their own thorny language. Having a name like Pipat Chumpol Ngarmchitr Chandrubeksa, as our guide did, must take its toll, too.

Pipat was built narrow as a pencil, and he moved with consummate grace. He could arch his fingers delicately backwards in the classical-dance hand positions, and his dark eyes were sorrowful, and his English was awful.

In the Chapel of the Emerald Buddha, I learned that a chapel was always a monastery, or else it was never a monastery but always a temple, or else never a temple . . . I couldn't quite make it out. In the early morning, put-putting down the *klong,* that large floating vegetable market, that cheerful bedlam of boats and barter and brown babies and broad, beaming smiles, I learned about water spinach, but not very much. ("Not know bo-*tonny,*" Pipat said sadly.) And about Thai breadfruit, which either cures gonorrhea or it doesn't. When Pipat told us with modest pride that he had been an inter-peter for a time at the U.S. military command there, I had a fresh insight into our country's problems in the Far East.

And I wondered then why travel books aren't more realistic. They keep coming out with the same old—if I may say it—clam juice: in the cities and larger towns, they insist, nearly everyone speaks English, when the truth is that hardly anyone does, outside the luxury shops and the big hotels, where they speak both English and Diner's Club equally well.

Or, to put it another way, the visiting American finds things about the same as the visiting foreigner does over here. I heard of a lost and lonely Frenchman in New York

who dived happily into a little shop on seeing its window
sign: ICI ON PARLE FRANÇAIS.

*"Qui est-ce qui parle français ici?"* he cried, at which a
fellow rushed in, beaming, from the back room. *"Je!"* said
he.

And so, in Amsterdam or Oslo or Tokyo or West Berlin,
just go across the street and around the corner to the little
place where you wanted to ask if the sandals are pigskin or
unborn water buffalo, and you find out that you can't find
out.

At this point, you generally unearth the Instant Language
Phrase Book. But it never heard of pigskin or water buffalo.
It gives you 'Good evening" or "Do you silage your maize?"
For no one within living memory has ever located a helpful
phrase in a phrase book when he needed it. And should he
actually find the one he wants—"Waiter, this soup is too
hot!"—the soup will need warming up again by the time he
has figured out how to pronounce it. Body language is better. Fan the soup. Set fire to your napkin. Cry.

The trouble is, phonetics aren't foolproof. In a Kyoto
temple one day, I saw some animal paintings done by a well-
meaning artist who had never seen the live animals, only
their dried, empty skins. They were the oddest-looking bears
and camels that ever happened, the accents in all the wrong
places and the shapes wrong, too, just as words come out
when they've been learned from a dead phonetic page.

For example, Temple Fielding points out in his *Travel
Guide to Europe* that before going to Austria you should
learn to say "Donkey fieldmice," because that is the phonetic
pronunciation for *Danke vielmals!*, meaning Thank you very
much! Or is for some people. But a Southern gentlewoman
I know would pronounce it *Doankih feemasse,* and I've no
idea what that means in German.

Or consider *derpty d'Asian nay,* which should get you two breakfasts in France. At any rate, that is the way I say *deux petits déjeuners,* and it works fine. But perhaps you pronounce *derpty d'Asian nay* differently.

I've noticed, too, that most French phonetics are too detailed (as I suspect all phonetics are, because everyone everywhere talks too fast). In France, the shopkeeper says, *"Au revoir, monsieur et madame,"* and the phrase book would give it at least six careful syllables. But what the shopkeeper really says is *"Vwahmssyer dom,"* which is never in the pronunciation guides.

It is accordingly with misgivings that I append a language guide of sorts to the end of this chapter, though I went to tremendous expense to get it, and Berlitz took great pains with it, too. Here are three valuable phrases phonetically translated into nineteen different languages, which leaves only four thousand nine hundred and eighty-one to go.

It is a start, though, and easy to use. You can point out the phrase to anyone who speaks the language—the guide, the stewardess, or the clerk in a big hotel—then listen carefully, and practice.

As to the phrases themselves, it wasn't easy to decide which to choose. "And mark it under ten dollars" was a strong contender, and so was "I was only kidding when I ordered this." I settled, finally, for the ones I've found handiest myself.

The first—"Is there someone around here who speaks English?"—at least explains your predicament; and the second—"Not just now, thank you"—can save you from getting into another one. It will dismiss, politely, the lady or gent who ardently desires to make your acquaintance when you are not feeling the same urge. Or someone who is about to serve you something you don't want to eat, or serve you more of what you already have enough of. Or someone who wants to take you somewhere you don't want to go or sell you something you don't want to own, like a big Oriental rug or a small Mexican lizard. ("Nice lizzer, lady? Lizzer shoes, lizzer belts? . . .")

The third phrase is the fast, no-fooling way of saying the same thing when they won't take no for an answer: "Go away! Beat it!" And perhaps it is the one to learn first.

*Mature people can be taught many things—speed reading, belly dancing, Serbo-Croatian—usually with much more pain, sweat, cost, time, and energy than most beginning pupils suspect.*

—AMITAI ETZIONI

*It may be better for humanity that we should communicate more and more. But I am a heretic, I think our ancestors' isolation was like the greater space they enjoyed: it can only be envied. The world is only too literally too much with us now.*

—JOHN FOWLES

*I wasn't worried; increasingly I find myself most comfortable with conversations I don't understand.*

—LILLIAN HELLMAN

# ARABIC

IS THERE SOMEONE AROUND HERE WHO SPEAKS
ENGLISH?
(*fee wa*-had houn *bih*-kee ink-*lee*-zee)

NOT JUST NOW, THANK YOU.
(Mish *hal*-la' *shuk*-ran)

GO AWAY (meaning, LEAVE ME ALONE)!
(Rouh min houn)

# CZECH

IS THERE SOMEONE AROUND HERE WHO SPEAKS
ENGLISH?
JE ZDE NĚKDO, KDO MLUVÍ ANGLICKY?
(ye zde nyegdoh gdoh mloovee anglitzky)

NOT JUST NOW, THANK YOU.
DĚKUJI, TEĎ NE.
(djekouyi tedj neh)

GO AWAY!
NEOBTĚŽUJTE MNE!
   (neh-ob-tje-jouy-te mne)

# DUTCH

IS THERE SOMEONE AROUND HERE WHO SPEAKS
ENGLISH?
IS ER IEMAND HIER DIE ENGELS SPREEKT?
(is ehr *eeh*-mahnd here deeh *eng-els sprayckt*)

NOT JUST NOW, THANK YOU.
NEEN DANK U, NU NOG NIET.
(nay dahnk ew new nogh neat)

GO AWAY!
GA WEG!
(khah vekh)

# FRENCH

IS THERE SOMEONE AROUND HERE WHO SPEAKS ENGLISH?
Y A-T-IL QUELQU'UN ICI QUI PARLE ANGLAIS?
(ee ah-teel kehl-kehng ee-see kee pahrl ongh-lay)

NOT JUST NOW, THANK YOU.
PAS MAINTENANT, MERCI.
(pah manh-tuh-nong, mare-see)

GO AWAY!
ALLEZ-VOUS EN!
(ah-lay voo zong)

# GERMAN

IS THERE SOMEONE AROUND HERE WHO SPEAKS ENGLISH?
SPRICHT HIER JEMAND ENGLISCH?
(sh'preekht here yeh-mahnt ehn-glish)

NOT JUST NOW, THANK YOU.
IM MOMENT NICHT, DANKE.
(im moh-ment nikht dahn-keh)

GO AWAY!
GEHEN SIE WEG!
(gay'n zee veck)

# GREEK

IS THERE SOMEONE AROUND HERE WHO SPEAKS ENGLISH?
(*ee*-nay kah-*nees* eh-*thoh poo* mee-*lah*-yee ahn-glee-*kah*)

NOT JUST NOW, THANK YOU.
(*oh*-khee *toh*-rah, ehf-khah-ree-*stoh*)

GO AWAY!
(*fee*-ghai ah-*poh* eh-*thoh*)

# HEBREW

IS THERE SOMEONE AROUND HERE WHO SPEAKS ENGLISH?
(mi-she-hoo me-da-ber po ang-leet)

NOT JUST NOW, THANK YOU.
(lo ah-shav to-dah)

GO AWAY!
(hys-talek me-po [masculine])
(hys-tal-kee me-po [feminine])

# HUNGARIAN

IS THERE SOMEONE AROUND HERE WHO SPEAKS ENGLISH?
BESZÈL ITT VALAKI ANGOLUL?
(beh-sail eeth vah-lah-kee on-gho-lool)

NOT JUST NOW, THANK YOU.
NEM MOST, KÖSZÖNÖM.
(nahm moshth kuh-suh-nuhm)

GO AWAY!
KÉREM HAGYJON BÉKÉBE!
(kaah-rehm hawd-yon baa-kaa-ben)

# ITALIAN

IS THERE SOMEONE AROUND HERE WHO SPEAKS ENGLISH?
C'E' QUI QUALCUNO CHE PARLA INGLESE?
(ch'*eh* kw*ee* kw*ahl*-koo-noh keh *pahr*-lah een-*gleh*-seh)

NOT JUST NOW, THANK YOU.
NON ADESSO, GRAZIE.
(nohn ah-*deh*-soh *grah*-ts'yeh)

GO AWAY!
SE NE VADA!
(seh neh *vah*-dah)

## JAPANESE

IS THERE SOMEONE AROUND HERE WHO SPEAKS ENGLISH?

KONO HEN NI EIGO O HANASU HITO GA IMASU KA?

(koh-noh hen nee eehee-go wo, hah-nah-soo hee-toh gah ee-mahss kah)

NOT JUST NOW, THANK YOU.

IMA DE NAKU, DOMO ARIGATO GOZAI MASU.

(*ee*-mah deh nak-kuh, doh-moh ah-ree-gah-toh goh-zahee mahss)

GO AWAY (meaning, LEAVE ME ALONE)!

ACCHI E ITTE!

(aht-chee eh eht-teh)

## MALAY

IS THERE SOMEONE AROUND HERE WHO SPEAKS ENGLISH?

ADA-KAH SIAPA-SIAPA DI-SINI YANG BOLEH BERBEHASA INGGRIS?

(aa-da-kah see-ya-pa see-ya-pa di-see-nee young bo-leh berb-ba-ha-sa ing-ge-ris)

NOT JUST NOW, THANK YOU.

BIAR DAHULU, TERIMA KASEH.

(bee-yar da-hu-lu te-ri-ma ka-seh)

*or*

TIDAK SEKARANG, TERIMA KASEH.

(ti-dak se-ka-rang, te-ri-ma ka-seh)

GO AWAY (meaning, LEAVE ME ALONE)!

JANGAN GANGU SAYA!

(ja-ngan gang-gu sa-ya)

*or*

PERGI!

(perr-gi)

## MANDARIN

IS THERE SOMEONE AROUND HERE WHO SPEAKS
ENGLISH?
Ts'eye[2] jeh[4] lee[3] foo[4] chin[1] yoo[1] mei[3] yoo[3] jen[3] hui[2] sho[2]
ying[2] wen[2] tee[4] ni[4]?

NOT JUST NOW, THANK YOU.
Pu[4] shih[4] kang[4] ts'ai,[1] hsieh,[3] hsieh[1] nee.[1]

GO AWAY (meaning, LEAVE ME ALONE)!
Tsou[4] k'ai[4]!
*and*

I DON'T WANT ANY!
Wǒ bù yau!

Numbers indicate tones
1: Normal tones (flat & short)
2: Said as if asking a question
3: Said as if asking Wh-a-a-a-t?
4: Said as if giving a command
(*Courtesy of the Berlitz Schools of Languages of America, Inc.*)

## PORTUGUESE

IS THERE SOMEONE AROUND HERE WHO SPEAKS
ENGLISH?
EXISTE ALGUÉM AQUI QUE FALA INGLES?
(ee-zeesh-chi algén á-keé kay fá-la een-glaysh)

NOT JUST NOW, THANK YOU.
AGORA NÃO, OBRIGADO (-A).
(ă-gó-ra nowń oh-bree-gah doo—*or* daa *if feminine*)

GO AWAY!
VÁ EMBORA!
(vá en-bó-ra)

## RUSSIAN

IS THERE SOMEONE AROUND HERE WHO SPEAKS ENGLISH?
(*yes*-lee *ktoh*-nee-bood *z'd'yehs ktoh* go-*vo*-reeth poh-an-*glee*-yskeey)

NOT JUST NOW, THANK YOU.
(n'yeh sehy-*cha*-s spa-*see*-boh)

GO AWAY (meaning, LEAVE ME ALONE)!
(e-*dee*-t' yeh prohch)

## SERBO-CROATIAN

IS THERE SOMEONE AROUND HERE WHO SPEAKS ENGLISH?
IMA LI NEKOG OVDE KO GOVORI ENGLESKI?
(e-mah lee *neh*-kog *ov*-deh *koh goh*-voree *ehn*-glehskee)

NOT JUST NOW, THANK YOU.
NE SADA, HVALA.
(*neh sah*-da *h'vah*-lah)

GO AWAY (meaning, LEAVE ME ALONE)!
OSTAVITE ME NA MIRU!
(o-*stah*-veeteh meh nah *mee*-roo)

## SPANISH

IS THERE SOMEONE AROUND HERE WHO SPEAKS ENGLISH?
¿HAY ALGUIEN AQUI QUE HABLE INGLES?
(eye ahl-g'yehn ah-kee keh ah-bleh een-glehs)

NOT JUST NOW, THANK YOU.
AHORA NO, GRACIAS.
(ah-oh-rah noh, grah-th'yahs)

GO AWAY!
VAYASE!
(vah-yah-seh)

## SWAHILI

IS THERE SOMEONE AROUND HERE WHO SPEAKS
ENGLISH?
KUNA MTU HAPA AMBAYE ANASEMA KIINGEREZA?
(koo-nah m'-too hah-pah ah-m'bah-yeh ah-nah-seh-mah
kee-ngheh-reh-zah)

NOT JUST NOW, THANK YOU.
SI SASA HIVI, ASANTE.
(see sah-sah hee-vee, ah-sah-ne-teh)

GO AWAY!
ENDA ZAKO!
(eh-n'dah zah-koh)

## TURKISH

IS THERE SOMEONE AROUND HERE WHO SPEAKS
ENGLISH?
BURALARDA İNGILIZCE KONUŞAN BIRISI VAR MI?
(bu-ra-lar-da in-gi-liz-dge ko-nu-shan bee-ree-see var-mu)

NOT JUST NOW, THANK YOU.
ŞIMDILIK HAYIR, TESEKKÜR EDERIM.
(shim-de-lek high-er te-shek-kur ede-rem)

GO AWAY (meaning, LEAVE ME ALONE)!
LÜTFEN BENI RAHATSIZ ETMEYIN.
(lut-fan be-nee ra-hat-suz et-me-yien)

## URDU-HINDI

IS THERE SOMEONE AROUND HERE WHO SPEAKS
ENGLISH?
K'YAH YAHAN PER KOI ADMI HAY JOE ENGLISH BOLTA HAY?

NOT JUST NOW, THANK YOU.
ABHI NAHIN, SUKRIYA.

GO AWAY (meaning, LEAVE ME ALONE)!
DHUR HATÒ!

# 8

---

# Lodgings

*Said the big fat lady with the wart on her nose,
"Mirror, mirror on the wall . . . ."*

Some travelers have a talent for landing every night in a cozy hotel where the decor is as charming as the landlord is friendly, where the omelets have to be strapped down so they won't go floating around the dining room, and where the drinks are this big.

But meanwhile, back at good old Cape Smiling, we take you to the Sherry-Hinterland, where anybody who is anybody stays, though by the time you've finished staying there you wish you were Somebody instead of anybody, because then you might be staying somewhere else.

You used to find plenty of writing paper there, in the flat middle desk drawer. Yes, and a pen that usually wrote, and a bunch of glorious free picture postcards, too, the building standing tall in proud isolation, the adjacent buildings disdainfully cut away.

No more. The writing paper and the postcards are long gone. Now you find a simple questionnaire and a printed note:

Dear Preferred Customer:

We sincerely appreciate your visit with us. Every effort has been made to provide you with the best. May we ask a favor?

In order to give you even better service, we would appreciate your answers to the following questions. Any additional comments and suggestions will be appreciated.

With many thanks,

Your Innkeeper

Well, I'd of answered, except I was too busy swatting flies.

What is the matter here? If he needs all that advice, why is he in the business? Why isn't he still back at hotel school or wherever it is they learn how to chain down the TV sets? (Like those menus that say "The chef invites your comments and suggestions." Does he really expect you to pay him a social call in the kitchen and ask constructive questions like What makes you think you can cook?)

My first suggestion to the Sherry-Hinterland is: Get some writing paper back into that drawer and get the questionnaires out of it. My second is: Let the hotel manager spend a week in this room himself and see how it grabs him. My third suggestion is: Tell the housekeeper to stay out of it while I'm in it.

"Just checking!" she hollers, with a great jangling of keys, as she opens, inexorably, the door.

Checking for what? Isn't there a house dick somewhere? Or anyway a button-eyed matron, presumably on the alert for hanky-panky? Hanky me no panky, dear, I'm not in the mood, not with that lady busting in all the time.

One time, gritting my teeth, I asked her, "Why do you *do* that?" (Why don't they assume you don't want to be disturbed till you indicate otherwise, instead of the other way around? Innocent till proven guilty.)

She answered, smug as the hangman who's going to do his duty if it kills you, "We have to find out if the room is still occupied."

Can't you assume it's occupied till I pay up and get out? I wanted to ask. In this age of sophisticated communications techniques, is this the best you can do?

But I didn't ask. I needed some more towels, and I didn't want to make the lady mad.

Yes, and my fourth suggestion—how much time have we got?—is: All together now, let's do something about the ghastly fluorescent lights in the bathroom that make the guest look on the verge of apoplexy or else freshly dug up. Or, as I remarked to my husband when he came in as I was brushing my teeth (he's the one with the purple nose and the green eyeballs), "YeeeoOWW!"

With me, this has been an enduring small crusade, right along with free toilets in airports. Those lights. I've mentioned the matter wistfully, hopefully, doggedly, despairingly, answering dresser-top questionnaire after questionnaire, always with the forlorn hope of somehow breaking through that glassy cybernetic wall. Get those lights out of here, I say. Please. And I sign and address it with care.

But the way of Preferred Customer is often hard.

Once upon a time, a man named Henry Llewellyn-Jones rode the crack train of its era from Chicago to New York. He dined well in the opulent dining car. (The dining car, children, was a car you used to see on trains, when you used to see trains. They specialized in good food and genially attentive service and spotless white napery starched vellum-smooth and heavy triple-plated silver eating tools, and fresh rosebuds on each and every table, and all this glory without bragging about it on the menu.)

Eventually, after a good cigar and an after-dinner high-ball in the club car, Mr. Llewellyn-Jones went to bed in his private bedroom, where he slept soundly through Ohio and most of Pennsylvania until he woke up scratching himself around Altoona, which is a very uncomfortable place to itch.

Here, there, and everywhere, he itched. And finally, on flashing his flashlight, he discovered what was the matter: bedbugs.

Well. Furious? He chewed out the porter, he leveled the conductor, and when he reached his office in New York that morning, he wrote a scorcher to the president of the railroad, who answered it the very same day.

"Dear Mr. Llewellyn-Jones," it began. "I know that no apology of mine for your most distressing experience on our train can begin to make up for the discomfort we have unknowingly caused you. The full price of your fare will, of course, be immediately refunded. Needless to say, this has never happened before, and you have my assurances that it will never happen again. Toward this end, I have seen to it that all passenger cars on the run will be taken apart, sterilized, and fumigated; all linen shall be disposed of . . ." et cetera, et cetera.

The letter was speeded to Mr. Llewellyn-Jones. But owing to a stenographer's oversight, it was stapled to Mr. Llewellyn-Jones's own letter of complaint, upon which the president had scribbled, "Send bedbug letter."

And so I had nearly despaired of accomplishing anything at all, in the matter of the bathroom lighting, till one day, in a lucid moment, I suddenly perceived what I should have perceived sooner: any filled-out questionnaire is undoubtedly tossed out, unread. (Why would a local manager with even a rudimentary brain forward these complaints to headquarters, only to be canned for his obvious incompetence?)

These questionnaires, I saw, are only a safety valve to

keep the guest from spitting on the walls or kicking the furniture.

That was the day I wrote a letter on my home typewriter to the chairman of a large hotel chain; and, eventually, I heard from him. He didn't get down to cases himself, but he delegated it to a presidential assistant who did. Because it seems to me that the exchange shows us both at our best, besides shedding some incandescence on the problem, I include the letters here.

Curtis L. Carlson, Chairman
Radisson Wichita
Wichita, Kansas

Dear Mr. Carlson,
It was my pleasure, for the most part, to stay recently at your Radisson Wichita Hotel, where I found the enclosed questionnaire. It has such a friendly sound that I thought you might answer my letter.
The subject is this: the ghastly fluorescent lights that are found in so many hotel and motel bathrooms, including—I am sorry to say—yours.
Perhaps you never shaved in front of one of your own hotel-bathroom mirrors, under that terrible light. As a woman, I never did either; but I have put on my make-up there, and I know of few things more shattering to the morale. These particular lights would be ideal for brain surgery. But I think they have no place in a hotel where any guest wants to believe that he is looking at least as presentable as he is. And your hotel-bathroom light is far more unkind than the

broad light of noonday, or even the notori-
ously cruel light of a cold winter dawn.

Can you tell me, please, why these lights
have been installed? They are not used in
other fine hotels, such as New York's Plaza
or the Algonquin, where one finds simple
incandescent lights that are nevertheless
more than adequate for anything a hotel
bathroom is apt to be used for.

As a writer, I am now at work on a travel
book, and I would like very much to be able
to explain the situation to my readers, in
case Mother buys a copy. May I have the
favor of a reply? A self-addressed envelope
is enclosed.

Sincerely,

Peg Bracken

Dear Miss Bracken,
We are very pleased that you enjoyed your
stay at the Radisson Wichita and hope that
you will find time to visit some of our other
Radisson Hotels located here in mid-America.
I have enclosed one of our brochures. • • •
Concerning the ghastly fluorescent lights in
Wichita and, as you say, throughout hotel and
motel bathrooms in the United States, there
is one theory for installing them and one
theory for not installing them. The "for"
theory is based on the fact that women in
particular prefer a strong light for make-up
purposes. I agree that fluorescents are
probably not the answer—and this is the

"against" theory—since they change the
color tones of the skin.
Many of the properties built when fluorescents were coming into their own installed
them because they were in vogue or the latest
thing at that time, and this included the
Radisson Wichita and, frankly, some of our
other properties. As we renovate guest-room
baths, the fluorescents are being phased
out. I feel that the ultimate in bathroom
lighting—at least related to mirror lighting—would be to have theatrical lights on
a rheostat so that the person using them
could turn them on and then adjust them to
the light level which they prefer. We are
considering this for some of our future
properties, depending on budget for instal-
lation and renovated baths.
Again, many thanks for your letter.

> Sincerely,
>
> Thomas S. Dawson
> Assistant to the President

It is nice to know that sometimes, somewhere, someone
will listen. Perhaps, someday, something will even happen.
"The longest journey begins with a single step"—Ling Po.
Or, possibly, Mao.

No matter. Back, now, to some terrible hotels.

Everyone needs a worst hotel in his life, I think—a place
to cherish and remember as the worst hotel in the world, so
that no matter how bad things get, he can always say to himself, Well, at least I'm not back at the good old El Puko.

However, in choosing the worst hotel, we must observe

certain rules; draw a clear line, that is, between the Rotten Hotel and the Old-fashioned Fleabag.

When you enter a hotel lobby of the general size and ambience of a bus-terminal rest room and, waiting to register, you find yourself behind a downy-cheeked sailor checking in with some overdeveloped lassie from some underdeveloped country, you sense that this is an honorable Old-fashioned Fleabag.

But don't knock it, we need it. Where else could the sailor go for four dollars and a half? Where else could my mother and I have gone? The city was bulging with two enormous conventions, and the Palace had lost our reservations, and it was 5:00 P.M. at the end of an eight-hour drive.

We didn't stay very long. The trouble was that nothing worked in our room except us, trying to open windows, shut doors, and, mainly, operate the plumbing. The toilet gushed when it shouldn't have and wouldn't gush when it should have, and Mumsie—she's the handy one—nearly caught the ague, up to her armpit that way in the icy waters of the tank.

However, when I say Rotten Hotel, I mean a hotel that is supposed to be a good one; a hotel with pretensions and prices to match; one to which the town's own citizens, who naturally don't know what they're talking about because they never stayed in it, will direct you with a clear conscience.

Unhappily often, this will be a motel—or so I've found on lecture tours—one of a vast peas-in-a-pod chain. Your hosts, embarrassed about the fusty great-aunt Mabel quality of the town's only hotel, book you in at the Imperial, the Royal, the Holiday Inn, the Hyatt, the Vagabond, the Whatever, but invariably in Exurbia, fourteen cornfields down the highway (though you came in on a plane).

WELCOME TO AMPAC CO.! the marquee says. And indoors, still smelling a bit of hot glue and new plasterboard, all the furniture sawed from some marvelous metal tree with a maple burl, or some marvelous plastic tree with an oak burl, everything colored gravy-tan or safe green or cream-cream, with Muzak pouring a relentless silver syrup over it all, this is the perfect place to write a book or sin with single-minded concentration or shoot yourself.

*Microscopic bars of gift-wrapped soap. Black plastic ashtrays. We are turtles and not travelers, and all over the world identical shells await us.*

—STEPHEN BECKER

In a Middle Western town, once, I was stuck by myself in the Ace Motel (or it might have been the Aztec or the Tropicana). It was seven miles out on U.S. 66, nothing to do but count the diesels go by, and it was truly unforgettable because of its remarkably high level of forgettableness.

The next morning, going through town on my way to make my speech, I noticed the old square six-story red brick Hotel President, right across from the Rialto.

I was curious: why hadn't the committee bedded me there? I'd have been within cozy reach of the drugstore, the bookstore, the newsstand, and Corinne's Salon de Beauté, not to mention Sears, Roebuck. And I asked my hostess, at the luncheon after the lecture, what the Hotel President was like.

Well, it was awfully—uh—small town, she explained, and she told me about the gentleman who had come to the hotel every weekday for forty-five years, formerly for lunch, but now that he was a very old gentleman indeed, only to sit in the lobby for an hour or two.

One cold January afternoon recently, she continued,

when she was waiting for a friend there, she asked the desk clerk if he'd mind shutting the front door, which was wide open, letting an icy wind whip in. He said he would shut it in a minute, after he'd aired the place. Once in a while, it seemed, the old gentleman wet his pants, but they didn't want to discourage his coming in, because he took such pleasure in his afternoons.

It showed a proper civic attitude, I thought, and I wished I had had the privilege of staying there, among such understanding folk, instead of in my sterile cookie-cutter cell on the outskirts of nowhere.

*"Oh, come off it!" Gunther Newton objected good-naturedly at this point. "Aren't you being a little . . . er . . . derivative?" (Gunther uses the polite word whenever he can.)*

*"How?" I said.*

*"You're maundering on like the ghost of Lucius Beebe or somebody," he said.*

*"Sometimes I get carried away," I admitted. "But that's what I mean."*

*"Is it? You mean you've never been glad to find a vacancy at a dependable brand-name motel?" he asked. "Never ran like a scared cat for a place you knew would be clean and the water hot and running, and a big stack of fresh, soft clean towels?"*

Well, his words stuck in my mind, as the truth so often will. Eventually, they nudged me into some rethinking and some backtracking, back to a wet night not long before, when I was forced down at a Howard Holiday (or some such) near the heliport where I'd left my car four days earlier, only an hour away from home. But driving the mountain road would have meant a long perilous sixty minutes through a wild rainstorm at ten o'clock at night at the wrong end of a rough trip.

So I checked in, and I loved every sterile, efficient, cozy, plastic minute of it, including the remote-control TV and a hot bath in a tub so clean it squeaked. Who needs picturesque servitors all the time, or old gentlemen wetting their pants in the lobby, either?

Also—for the record—I had an interesting conversation with the coffee-shop waitress when she brought my clam chowder. Looking around, I'd estimated that a sizable herd of Naugas had given their all to the comfortable dark-blue upholstered booths, and I'd noticed, too, that the plastic ferns in the long planter box needed dusting. I don't know why I can't keep my mouth shut about the plants in restaurants, for my own are no great shakes at home. Anyway, I mentioned it.

The waitress didn't seem offended. She was a friendly girl, with a round face and two big front teeth like a cheerful beaver's. "I know," she said. "We're getting around to that. Today we dusted the wall things." She pointed to some armorial shields hanging there, molded of some dark brown plastic, like coagulated cocoa.

"You know," she continued conversationally, "some people don't like those plastic plants. A lady asked just the other day why we don't have real ones. But I told her, I said if we had real ones we'd have bugs, too, and then we'd have to use spray, and, you know, with food and all—" I could see she'd had the proper ecological upbringing.

"And then you girls would have to spend a lot of time talking to them, too," I said. I had recently been reading about how sensitive the green growing things are, and how they thrive on chitchat, except for weeds, which seem to thrive anyway.

She nodded. "I know," she said. "I have a couple of plants this fellow gave me in my room [she lived in San Francisco], and he said I should talk to them and they'd bloom better. But I felt kind of silly. I mean, what do you say? You know? So finally—I live at the corner of Bush and Jones—it just came to me, how to do it. I named one of them Bush and the other one Jones. So now, when I come in after work, I usually water them, and I always say 'Hello, Bush! Hello, Jones!' . . ."

I've wondered ever since how Bush and Jones and the waitress are doing.

But back to the main highway now, and a good question: What is the worst hotel I know? Of all the impossible *posadas,* lugubrious lodgings, and horrendous hotels I ever stayed in, which is the absolute nadir?

Of course, there is no one true answer. So much depends on the mood and the moment. Too, I find that I must limit the contenders to the continental United States, because elsewhere I tend to confuse the crummy with the picturesque. (Hawaiian smog doesn't really taste any better than other kinds, and yet it seems to, when it is part volcanic and they christen it vog.)

Certainly there is no shortage of awful hotels abroad, a fact well known to anyone who starts out with more enthusiasm than reservations. I remember one near Windsor Castle that would have been snooted by the more fastidious bacteria, and an equally colorful Red youth hostel in Czechoslovakia (I don't know why I was there, either) with one candle stub to read by, and a small public front yard as its only plumbing. I also remember a true hellhole on the Mediterranean, a *sac de puces* called the "Calanques," where the beach was almost as oily as the pillowcases, and the blankets were too thin for dishtowels, and the waiter's nose ran but not the waiter, and the only bright spot was reflecting that if the owners ever produced a daughter they could name her Klinkety.

Yet memory overlays even these with a thin magic, for they were (as they say in little Scottish border towns) *they* places, not here places. I must look nearer home. And after all, deciding isn't too hard, for there emerges one dreary common denominator of all truly rotten hotels: an impenetrable indifference. Nobody cares, and you know it.

With this the criterion, then, I award the cast-iron mattress to a semi-Olde-English establishment in Atlantic City, one of those queasy hotel-motel compromises that combine the more uncomfortable features of each. It is one of a large chain, all quaintly named; we'll call it "Ye Flabby Arms." (Names have been changed to protect the writer.)

This particular trip had started out lumpily and kept on going downhill. Though I didn't know it then, it was a good example of Gunther Newton's Theory of Irreversibility. Some time ago, he figured out that every trip has a certain built-in tilt, up or down. Like a love affair, he said—or a batch of hollandaise, Mrs. Newton threw in—once it starts to curdle, there isn't much to be done besides fasten the seat belt and hang in there.

A couple of hours out of San Francisco, we force-landed in Denver with engine trouble, and in the airport coffee shop I saw a woman wearing my own identical new suit. Brand-new heathery tweeds, ours were, with a pink fleck, and I was fond of mine. Had been.

Eventually, they let us board some other airplane, one of the pilot models from Pitch Roll & Yaw, and on it I happened to sit beside a woman wearing a grandmother bracelet. When I saw those seven gold disks, I knew it was going to be a long day's journey. And I was right, though presently

I had more interesting things to worry about, because somewhere over Missouri, they told us to assume the crash position: lean forward, head on the knees—back to the womb, or somewhere.

Well, nothing happened. But afterward, we felt like old friends, the lady and I, and we discussed a number of things —among them, how long we wanted to live. There's nothing like the crash position for getting you down to brass tacks.

She said she'd like to live awhile longer, all right, but not long enough to watch her children come apart too much. She told me about an eighty-seven-year-old friend of hers who had had to drive her sixty-five-year-old daughter down to get her new dentures (the daughter's), because the daughter had had three tickets for speeding and lost her license about the same time as her teeth. You should move along, my new friend said, before things like that start to happen.

The daughter sounded like a real swinger to me—three tickets for speeding at her age—although I could see the lady's point. And you couldn't call it an invigorating conversation. So when we landed at Atlantic City, I was anticipating with pleasure my snug, solitary berth at the hotel, though I had to settle for a cold lonely stroll down the Boardwalk in the gathering January dusk because my room at Ye Arms wasn't ready.

Casual workmen had just finished pounding some new boards into the classic herringbone weave of the Walk. The new wood was raw orange against the weathered gray of the old, and the smoggy and sand-sky-ocean stretched, a nonstop dishwater yellow, and a sharp wind stabbed my ankles as I plodded past the souvenir shops. The ones that weren't boarded up were full of salt-water taffy in heaps, sacks, boxes, and quaint plastic barrels, or else they featured those bouffant multicolored nylon-petal hats. Only shortly before, I had seen those hats all over Hawaii but assumed they were safely quarantined there along with the pineapple thrip.

Well, no matter. I'd feel better, I knew, back at the hotel, where I could jump into a hot toddy and a hot bath in about that order. But I hadn't reckoned on the bar, closed for re-modeling, along with the coffee shop, or the new night clerk. He had considerable hair growing out of his ears, the way Pullman conductors do, and he'd have made a good one, for it was clear that he hated everybody and didn't care if they hated him back or not. People like this seem to win all the battles, though they may lose the war. Or maybe they've already lost it and that's why they act that way, I don't know. Anyway, they all end up working for some railroad or some hotel in Atlantic City.

Ye Flabby Arms was a place that made you feel at home, inasmuch as nobody listened to you and you carried your own bag. The bellhop was somewhere else, though I nearly fell over him later that night on a stair landing (the elevator had quit, too), slumped behind the daily *Scream,* a half-peeled, half-chewed Butterfinger gripped in his fist like a banana.

I never saw the bellhop hop, though he proved ambulatory when I was trying to get a candy bar out of the lobby machine, which kept coughing up the dime. This, it developed, was because the machine was unplugged. Well, naturally—as the bellhop pointed out, ambling over—there was no wall outlet on that side of the room. But, as he elaborated further, this didn't really matter, because all the slots were empty except for the Cheez-'n'-Crax. I didn't feel like Cheez-'n'-Crax.

My room, too, was full of surprises. Done in subtle shades of rat-beige and gangrene, it smelled of mold, fish, salt water, and nine thousand previous weary occupants. The bathroom boasted not only a broken toilet but a matched set of bathtub faucets so sharp you had to wear a washcloth like a mitten, but there weren't any washcloths. In a word, nothing had been overlooked for the discomfort and inconvenience of the guest.

However, in one of a chain like this, you can always read in the house magazine (right there on top of the TV) about the glories of its other hotels you are not in. There is the Knight's Reste in Nassau, with its cozy Guinevere Bar and the fabulous Sky Lounge. And Ye King's Keep (Denver), with its world-famous Beef 'n' Truffle Restaurant and its mammoth rooms with the huge down puffs the guests disappear into, after an exhilarating day on the ski slopes. Or the honeymoon package deal in California (Ye Randy Princess), where you get a bonus of free booze and fruit (citrus only) in three days' and two nights' revelry, plus a gold-trimmed certificate, certifying exactly what, they don't say, but suitable for framing. But that isn't the hotel you happened to hit. And you're not on a honeymoon, Maude.

I know that some people say you should always ask to see another room if you're shown to the mother-in-law room or, more accurately, if the mother-in-law room is shown to you.

"Do you really expect me to stay in this dump?" you ask your friendly innkeeper, when you arrive at 10:00 P.M. Then he can answer with perfect courtesy, "Not at all, sir or madam as the case may be, I recommend that you go somewhere else."

And this is exactly what I'm afraid would happen. Unlike the people who tell you to do that, I never feel that I'm playing from a position of strength. Clout is what I feel the need of. Travel agents and Ari Onassis and people with Vuitton luggage are full of clout. But at this point I'm only full of airplane bordelaise and a certain stoic calm.

And there's something else: after all, this creep is, in a sense, my host. You can't tell your host that his place is a disaster. I wasn't reared that way. So how do you get out of it? Tell him it looks great, just the place for getting over your pyromania? Or ask if he's sure your ballet practice won't bother anybody, and go into a couple of fast *entrechats,* and he'll think you're balmy. . . .

I stay, which proves it.

I don't believe I'll even mention here the forbidding mechanical aspects of the thoroughly modern hostelry, except to say that nonmechanically minded people have an increasingly harder time of it each passing year.

Recently, my husband and I stayed in a motel equipped with a "Magic Fingers" box between the twin beds. "It quickly carries you into the land of tingling relaxation and ease," the sign said, twenty-five cents for fifteen minutes.

We thought there were more natural and even cheaper ways of achieving the same thing, so we didn't bother with it, though we learned later of a couple who did. They dropped a quarter in, but nothing happened because (they learned later) the power had gone off. It came back on with a great jiggling surge at three in the morning, when they were sound asleep, scaring them halfway into the hall.

Then there are the Sani-wrapped glasses and the Bacteriostatic soap. Yes, and there is the proud *"Desinfectada!"* printed on the paper strip around the toilet seats in some Mexican places. (This side of the border it says only "Sanitized for Your Safety," which isn't half so thrilling.)

Though I've never had the privilege of watching the disinfecting ceremony, I'm sure it's a ring-tailed stemwinder, probably like the changing of the guard.

In my mind's eye I can see the spray-gun crew marching smartly in, three or four of the country's finest—tall, erect, clear-eyed, white-suited, masked—and hear the staccato commands: "Ready—aim—watch it, men, stand back—

FIRE!" And then the moment of truth, taut as a fiddlestring, breaths bated for the final security-purity check. Then the long, slow exhalations, and the paper strip deftly applied, before the lads stride out again, shoulder to shoulder, chests out, another job well and truly done.

And yet, I'm not sure I'd want to watch the operation, after all. If I had been the previous guest, it would hurt my feelings, though not quite so cruelly, at that, as the bizarre goings-on at the Hotel Bristol, in Paris.

The Bristol is an extraordinarily lavish and lovely hotel on the Rue du Faubourg-St.-Honoré, where I stayed once in a splendid cherry-velvet-and-ivory suite just long enough to learn that I couldn't afford it. I didn't know it at the time, but I have learned since that every single toilet seat is individually removed, scraped, and revarnished after each guest leaves and before the arrival of the next.

It is just as well that I didn't know about this while I was there, for I would have felt more nervous than I already was. It always bothers me to think that my host has gone to so much trouble. Anyway, I've never quite trusted those quick-drying varnishes.

## House Rules at the Pioneer Inn
### *Lahaina, Maui, Hawaii*

You must pay you rent in advance.
You must not let you room go one day back.
Women is not allow in you room.
If you wet or burn you bed you going out.
You are not allow to gambel in you room.
You are not allow to give you bed to you freand.
If you freand stay overnight you must see the mgr.
You must leave you room at 11 a.m. so the women can
    clean you room.
Only on Sunday you can sleep all day.

You are not allow in the down stears in the seating room
or in the dinering room or in the kitchen when you
are drunk.
You are not allow to drink on the front porch.
You must use a shirt when you come to the seating room.
If you cant keep this rules please dont take the room.

## 2

*In all first-class hotels the visitor has a right to ex-
pect a high degree of comfort; and he need have no
hesitation in requiring such small conveniences as
hot water in the morning and before table d'hote, an
abundant supply of towels, pen and ink in his bedroom, etc. In hotels not lighted throughout with gas
there should be a supply of bedroom-candles on
every floor, and not merely at the foot of the stair-
case. . . .   —KARL BAEDEKER, 1890*

Consider, for a moment, the hotels and motels you've stayed
in, then marvel at the adaptive machinery of the brain! Consider its automatic print-out of the data necessary to get you
out of or back to the room—up nine floors, down a long
hall, sharp right to the broom closet under the exit sign,
sharp left to No. 455—all on invisible tape that self-de-
structs three seconds after you turn in your key.

Yet the feel of them remains. And you like some and remember them vividly for various deep-seated reasons you
probably shouldn't examine too closely or you might learn
something.

A woman under a neighboring hair drier in Hong Kong
told me that she loved the accommodations thus far on her

tour. Each hotel had been either a Hilton or an Inter-Continental; and there was always so much doing in them, she said, that she and her husband hadn't had to go outside at all.

And some travelers stick with peas-in-a-pod motels, because they hate learning a new shower every night and they know exactly where to find the ice machine.

And some enjoy the off-chance of seeing the Aga Khan at the Ritz in Paris, or the blither spirits who prowl the halls at the Algonquin in New York. Or they like the music and talk and paint that seeps between the floor boards at New York's Chelsea, or the feeling that there'll always be an England that they get at Brown's, in London, reaffirmed with every clank of the lift.

The Chinese have a good phrase—*Bun chi yu kwai*—which means the feeling of returning home. (Home, here, means the place you'd rather be than anywhere else, though unfortunately this isn't always where you live.) Ideally, it means an all-over welcoming warmth, which is the first consideration with many people—the warm personal greeting, not so much from the smiling manager, who keeps an efficient guest-card index, but from the elevator boy, who actually remembers them.

To me, hotels are always female, as boats are, and hurricanes. There are all kinds: country lasses and Barbie dolls, high-priced call girls and cozy grandmas; society broads who try too hard and sluts who don't try hard enough and *grandes dames* who must be lived up to and raddled old actresses pawing over their raddled old clippings. . . . Somehow it is generally the country girl that I like the best, and the snug tatty grandma.

The first hotel I liked was in Xenia, Ohio, a Sherwood Anderson sort of a place near the college I wanted to be graduated from. In order to do so, it was necessary to write one of those what-college-done-for-me papers; and I felt the need of anonymous surroundings for the job, away from the dormitory. So I moved in for a few days with my typewriter.

It was a two-storied red brick place with a big vertical corner sign:

H
O
T
E
L

which referred only to its second story, the street floor being half bakery, half poolroom. But it fulfilled my requirements —kept me warm, sheltered, and private, at a price in line with its modest facilities, though I never knew whether the bed was comfortable or not, because every time I was in it I was asleep. I wrote the paper rather quickly there and it had loomed as a horrendous job, so I've kept kindly memories of the place ever since.

Another fine hotel I think of promptly when the subject arises is in North Dakota—Bismarck's Grand Pacific Fantasy Hotel, one of the world's endangered species, and therefore the more appealing. Once upon a time, I stayed there.

Homy as meat loaf but not so slow for all that, the Fantasy was a gutsy old girl, with her hair dyed black, and a new set of snow-white clackers. She was 1971 Plastic Tubular out of 1920 Golden Oak Railroad Functional and on her toes, yes *sir*.

When my husband and I arrived late that night, we went behind the J. C. Penney island window to find the entrance to the small dark lobby. Inside, to the right, was a bulletin board loud with coming attractions: cattle auction, Baptist church services, wrestling match (Mad Dog Cochino versus Bad Boy Bullenski) and—because I was speaking at the town hall the next day—me.

To the left was the scarred oak reception desk, more pigeonholes than pigeons, and a genial desk clerk, delighted to see us, glad we made it, how was the trip, didn't we need something to eat. And there was a comfortable lived-in smell. Neither cabbage and spittoon, nor air freshener and formaldehyde. Just comfortable.

So we climbed a skinny stair to a skinny hallway thinly carpeted in something rosy, the contact pleasantly intimate between the bones of the feet and the bones of the floor, and went on down to No. 27, our suite. Suite, mind you, not just a room, but a suite you could swing a heifer in, with an ice-box full of beer and orange pop, and the whole place alive with personal touches, not one of them chained down.

Yellow rubber chrysanthemums sprang from green glass sand! Beautiful dead butterflies reposed in shadowbox frames! Kipling's "If," magnificently curlicued by an ardent calligrapher, held down the west wall! And the old high ceilings had been cozily lowered and the catsup-colored bed-spreads glowed, and so did the thick red curtains hiding the big windows (which actually opened). Someone had liked it and done his very best. Good vibes.

Snow fell that night, as softly enveloping as the mattress we bundled on. Next morning was cold, till the radiator clanked up a German schottische, and when we worked up enough nerve to try the Sudden Room Service for breakfast (would they lob it in from the hall?), the desk clerk brought it in five minutes. Same desk clerk, with fresh orange juice, hot rolls, and good coffee strong enough to walk a mouse on.

"She's gettin' warmer," he said cheerfully. "Up to twenty

already." I thought of that fine opening line in *Mrs. Wiggs,* "The thermometer's done fell up to zero," as he bustled about, pulling the red curtains to admit some of the snowy dazzle.

We could have hibernated till June there. It seemed a sorry trade, exchanging North Dakota for Southern California, our next stop, where the air tasted like an old cigar butt, under a sky the color of a mild bruise.

And so, as we've noted, preferences are personal. To me, hotels mean shelter, and something to be sheltered *from,* a definition that strikes out the sunny smiling places where being indoors is a penance, no matter how lush the indoors is. Those places are resorts or clubs or island paradises, but they aren't, precisely, hotels.

And I think of companionableness, which narrows the choice still further to a hotel or an inn, somewhere in the British Isles, with a snug lounge-bar where a traveler can swap lies with another, in a reasonably similar tongue. You can become intimate quickly, not in spite of the brevity of the encounter, but because of it, and because you'll not be seeing your new friend again. (There's hardly a thing you couldn't confide, under those circumstances.)

There are two inns I especially remember, the first in Scotland. We'd driven that day through October country the color of pheasant feathers, then stopped at sundown at an inn in the village of Crianlarich. In the small lounge-bar, classically and cozily dark-paneled, red-papered, and glinting with brass, a few of us sat around a bright coal fire, while the savory smell of roasting lamb curled in from the kitchen.

While my husband shaved upstairs, I read the Edinburgh paper and chatted with a small Scot in a shabby suitcoat and shiny trousers. He wanted to know what I was about, and I told him I'd been looking for bracken that day on the hillside, as I had, but it was nearly November now, and late in the season.

"If ye'd come two weeks ago we'd ha' paid ye to pick it," he said cheerfully, and told me they made a great dish in the springtime. You take the bracken fiddleheads and bring them to a boil twice, for the bitterness, then serve them with margarine and salt. It sounded a little south of scrumptious, I thought, but still it's good to know these things; and so I thanked him before he finished his ale and chugged off. For the first time, then, I really noticed the stout cheerful woman sitting across the hearth.

Stout isn't a fashionable word, but neither was she a fashionable woman. Her perm had frizzed, and her brown wool suit was touched with brown satin. Dressmaker suit, they'd have called it back in the days when clothes were worn oftener and longer—through a predictable downhill run from best to second-best to everyday to working-around-the-house-in.

She was tatting away at a half-finished sunburst doily, and when the phone rang in the room beyond, she jumped and nearly dropped it. She gave me an apologetic look.

"It's just I'm always thinking it's for me," she said.

I know the feeling. I often have it when a telephone rings, even in an unlikely place.

But her reasons were sounder than mine, it developed, as she told me about a strange time in her life—a bad one, too. Her husband had finally died after a hard, old two years in hospital and out, she said, and there was a terrible go-round about insurance, and then if her twelve-year-old didn't up and break his leg, and her working all day in a bakeshop.

What happened was this: she was in a shoe-repair place,

stocking feet, cobbler putting heels on her shoes, when the phone rang in the back room and a woman's voice yelled, "You got a Mrs. Loralee Barnes?"

That was her name, and so she stocking-footed it back behind the counter into the cluttered parlor, wondering, Who knew she was there? Hadn't known she'd be there herself, till she popped in the door.

"Loralee?" said a pleasant voice. "This is God."

And *she* said (this is what she'll never get over, not if she lives to be a thousand)—"God who?"

"Your good friend God," the voice said. "I just want you to know you're doing fine, Loralee. And don't you go worrying about Ritchie's leg now. It's going to be good as new."

Well, talk about floored! Of course she was.

"You didn't recognize the voice at all?" I asked.

She shook her head. "Never heard it before in my life," she said. But this was only the beginning. Every week, sometimes once, maybe twice, but every week, she said impressively, for anyway six months, He'd call, sometimes when she was home but more often not. Once at an East End Lyons, just stopped in for a bite. And there. The phone rang. Once in a waiting room, some hospital where she'd taken some night clothes for a neighbor. Here, there, anywhere. Just a few words, but always something encouraging, something nice.

"He'd know when I was worried about a furniture payment, and the time I had the infected ear, and when mother got so sick. . . ." She tatted away. The doily was growing briskly.

"Did you ever try to have a call traced?" I asked.

"Yes. I did. But I—" She stopped and started again. "Well, you see, of course I didn't *believe* it, if you know what I mean. But still I didn't exactly *not* believe it—you know? And so, that once, when I asked Operator if she could trace it, I knew right then I didn't want to know, even if she could. So I said, Never mind. . . ."

The last call had come about two years ago, she said. Not that He said it was the last call. He just didn't call any more. And things have been going all right ever since. She had married again— And just then he came into the lounge-bar. He was a solid, good-natured man, with a fringe of ginger hair around his otherwise bald head and lively blue eyes; and he wore a knitted gray vest under his brown suit, standard practice in Scotland in the fall.

They were a comfortable couple and obviously pleased with each other. I was glad everything had worked out so well.

Then there is an English place I would like to mention— another inn I remember with enduring affection—where I stayed for a week in Extremis (somewhere near Woking, I believe). I'd stopped in to have the flu, one snowy late February, after a cold trek around Ireland.

It was more pub than inn, only three rooms to let. Mine had a key big enough to lock a castle, and a square-shouldered pewter hot-water bottle, and the armoire would have held six bodies. Great purple pansies galloped around the top of the wallpaper, picking up speed as my fever went up, slowing when it dipped.

The village doctor who examined me did so with remarkable thoroughness. He even asked me all about my sex life, which seemed rather unprofessional of him, just for a case of flu, and I remember thinking, It's no wonder they call these British doctors Mister. But mainly I remember lying there watching the gentle snow soften the landscape and heap itself to a high ridge on the Watney's Ale board hung just outside my window.

Somewhere out there under the cold ground, all the primroses were sleeping, which was sensible of them. And I could see a bird's nest high in the tall bare tree across the road. A rook's nest, probably. When the rooks nest high, it means a hot summer coming. The chubby bar girl who kept my hot-water bottle filled had told me that. And I remember burrowing into the deep, heavenly, enveloping warmth of bed and blankets, sipping a little Scotch, and successfully quelling the wild urge to go lope through another castle.

*No one can describe the delight of coming to a sudden drop and looking down into a rich wooded valley where you see the roofs of the place where you're going to have supper and bed; especially if the sunset lies on the ridge beyond the valley. There is so much mixed in it; the mere physical anticipation, as of a horse nearing his stable, the sense of accomplishment and the feeling of "one more town," one further away into the country you don't know, and the old, never hackneyed romance of travelling.* —C. S. LEWIS

# 9

---

# Some Things to Bring

| Beasts of burthen: | lbs. |
|---|---|
| *An ass will not usually carry more than about* | *65* |
| *A small mule* | *90* |
| *A horse* | *100* |
| *An ox of average breed* | *120* |
| *A camel* (*which rarely can be used by an explorer*) | *300* |

—FRANCIS GALTON

Last spring at Orly airport, I was waiting in the queue at the counter marked "Douane," forty minutes before planetime. It is here that they validate the papers giving people a rebate on the pretty odds and ends they blew their francs on at the American Express shop around the corner from the Opéra. I was second in line, behind a solid Lebanese man with an attaché case.

Behind us the queue lengthened rapidly, everyone with a plane to catch and all of us clutching our passports and papers. A warm slow current of rage rippled down the line like wind through wheat as M. le Douanier did his yesterday's homework, never lifting his constipated little face for a glance in our direction.

In methodical slow motion, he stamped his foot-high stack of papers, folded each and every one with exquisite care, and tucked it thoughtfully into an envelope. The minutes ticked by. Around us, the rest of the airport buzzed, bustled, and roared. Outside, the big jets zoomed for home. But here, life had stopped. Ten minutes. Fifteen. Twenty-five minutes. Finally, I tried, hopelessly: *"Monsieur, s'il vous plaît . . ."*

He didn't look up. Lift. Stamp. Fold. Insert. Lift. Stamp. Fold. Insert. Clearly, *il ne plaisait pas.*

My vibrations apparently reached the Lebanese gentleman in front of me. He spoke then, though barely turning his head. I could see only the smooth Buddha-like curve of his cheek.

"Patience, madame," he murmured.

"Where do you get some?" I asked.

"You bring it from home," he said.

He was right, of course. I should have thought of it sooner.

However, I have thought a good deal since then about the mussy matter of packing, and I have come to some conclusions.

Next to patience, in the order of importance, comes a good all-around credit card. Then, after that:

Something readily edible in the pantry or the freezer for the first night home, unless you live over a delicatessen;

Your passport number, securely inside your head, for it's as easy as a phone number and saves rummaging later on;

Extra money in some awkward form that isn't too easy to cash. A foreign-currency draft is good, and they're available at some banks—ask your banker. These are usually cheaper than traveler's checks but cashable only at a specific bank or its branches during banking hours. This is mainly insurance for possible crises, like a lost plane ticket or finding a lovely leather coat in Seville* and you may not be back that way.

---

* It is highly probable the leather-coat man will accept the credit card, but there are still some little shops and good craftsmen who don't.

The first thing to do in packing a suitcase is remove the gnir with a vacuum cleaner or a small whisk broom. As Robert Benchley defined it, gnir is, or are, the little woolly particles found in the bottom of pockets, especially constructed for adhering to candies. Gnir adheres to the inside of suitcase pockets, too. Ideally, one should have removed it after unpacking the last time, but one seldom does.

What kind of suitcase depends, of course, on the kind you have. Each has its advantages, except for the enormously expensive kind, which the help loves to kick, and still they expect you to tip more. Like babies, it isn't the initial cost of these beauties, it's the upkeep.

I know a woman who bought three bags and a shoe case and five kitchen utensils (her choice) plus a miniature orange tree, all for $29.95, and has traveled happily with them for several years, everything except the tools and the orange tree.

A fold-over Val Pack is good for a tall person, but on a short person it can bump and stub along most uncomfortably.

The flat linen-chest kind makes it easier to find your belongings, assuming they are there, because it can be packed in layers. A good system is to cut a sheet of corrugated cardboard to fit, then first pack in the bottom what you won't need too often. Put the divider on top, then the rest of the gear. This way you can remove the top layer on its tray without stirring things up.

Impatient people who hate waiting at baggage carrousels prefer a fold-over garment bag that stays with them on the plane. If there isn't room in the airplane closet, it can ride on the shelf over the seat.

As for feminine packing, an unbiased survey of two and a half million women shows that the sensible ones leave dresses, jackets and skirts on wire hangers, in Pliofilm dry cleaner's bags. Then in smaller plastic bags, they group the smaller items, except for something made of patent leather, because Pliofilm ruins its shine.

As for men, I don't know what they do, I only know that you shouldn't do it for them if you can help it. Everyone should have the privilege of forgetting his own underwear.

*Now that our marriage has survived the joys of travel, we're certain that it can survive just about anything.* —JUDITH VIORST

Another thing to avoid at all costs is the Camel System of packing, so-called because of Roasted Bedouin Camel, which is supposedly the world's largest single dish. For special occasions, the Bedouin stuffs cooked eggs into fish, and the fish into cooked chickens, and the chickens into a roasted sheep carcass, and finally, with a mighty shove, stuffs the whole thing into a whole camel. As a result, they can't find much of anything over there.

The big problem in packing a bag this way (the flask rolled up in the underpants that are stuck in a shower cap that's jammed into a raincoat pocket) is that—as in long division—you generally forget what goes into what and do it differently each time. If there is one thing the traveler eventually learns, it is the importance of packing and repacking his suitcase the same way every time so he can locate his Alka-Seltzer in the dark the way a soldier can assemble his rifle. It is true that the traveler usually trips over something in the dark on the way to his suitcase and wakes up everyone anyway. But the principle is still sound.

Marking is important, too. You want your name and address inside your bag, preferably pasted on the underside of the lid, should the outside tag come off and the bag go to Cairo though you don't. And, of course, the outside should be outstanding in some fashion. Now that travelers outnumber bag styles, it's easy to grab the wrong suitcase full of clothes that probably wouldn't fit anyway. Too, there is always something so unappetizing about the contents of some stranger's suitcase, all those wadded-up intimate-looking things. Customs men and agricultural-inspection men must have depressing dreams.

So spray-lacquer the suitcase handle in some violent color, or paste a fluorescent butterfly on the bag, or attach a squirrel tail—something.

What goes into the bag is, of course, an individual matter. Certainly, a trip can be nearly ruined by forgetting one small, individual, and highly essential thing. I don't mean the sort of thing that comes in those bon-voyage gift kits full of tiny items you already have around the house. The other day I saw one advertised that sounded like the contents of a giant Boy Scout's pocket:

| | |
|---|---|
| pill bottles | clips |
| Scotch tape | rubber bands |
| rain bonnet | sewing kit |
| shower cap | pins |
| plastic hanger | cup |
| raincoat | antacid tablets |
| liquid shampoo | aspirin |
| soap | knife, spoon, fork |
| 2 towelettes | Band-Aids |
| matches | note pads |
| comb | pencils |

| spot remover | tags, labels |
| tissues | emery board |

For $6.95 I thought they could have included a pair of scissors, which are always handy, too: It's rather like the Vermont storekeeper who advertised his "Big Free Bonus-Gift Day." With each ten-dollar purchase, the customer would receive a free cigarette lighter and a pants hanger, which turned out to be a match and a nail.

By one essential thing, I mean something like your Dramamine or your worry beads or your favorite putter or your hair dye. (Another brand of Peach Chiffon might be more of a Halloween orange.) Or the home-polished agate cuff links that accompany a man I know everywhere but fishing, and if he unaccountably forgets to pack them, he mourns.

Another friend of mine wouldn't cross a county line without her Swiss army knife, with its screwdriver, bottle opener, can opener, awl, scissors, corkscrew, big blade, little blade, nail file—nine great little tools for the size of one. My own essential, which I pack first, is a thick engrossing book; and I make sure it is engrossing to me before I pack it.

I know a photographer's wife who takes along a lightweight folding camp stool if they so much as go around the corner, I suppose for those long time-exposures. And a reporter who carries along a hundred-watt bulb for reading in European hotel bedrooms. She finds that it works in the American-oriented hotels there. (If it doesn't, I suppose she goes out and buys one that does.)

I never researched this, because I usually pack a battery lamp. These are hard to find in stores, but you can get one for about seven dollars from a place called Travelers Checklist, 307 Fifth Avenue, New York, N.Y. 10016. It improves many a U.S. hotel room, too. So often, the choice is between the ten-watt bulb on the ceiling and the three-hundred-watt lamp between the beds.

Too, a vacuum hook is good to have along for many European bathroom doors. Otherwise there is no place to hang a robe or anything else. Especially French bathroom doors. *Regardez, Maman! Mes panty hose sont tombés dans le bidet!* And remember the merits of an inflatable camping pillow when the hotel's own are few and skimpy.

In fact, preparing for a hotel room's probable deficiencies makes rather a hefty packing category all its own. Take the matter of noise.

Once I was registering at a middle-size town's de-luxe hotel at the same time a bride and groom were. I could tell they were Just Married because the rice kept falling out of her veil, and it turned out that they had the room right next to mine, as well as a very nice honeymoon, only two inches away. (They don't build hotel-room walls the way they used to.)

On the other hand, you sometimes wish you had some earplugs along, especially when you're staying at motels. Sometimes you're too close to the noisy highway, or not far enough from the Sombrero Room, where they stomp on Mexican hats all night.

According to those who know their earplugs, *Boules Quies* are quite effective. They are pellets of some odd pliant pink wax, especially available in Paris and London, but probably in some U.S. pharmacies, too. If not, other kinds are.

Then there is the matter of binoculars, or opera glasses. Not being a bird watcher, I don't customarily have them along. But I remember the time I just happened to—a pair of very small opera glasses, more for operettas, in Acapulco.

After discovering their all-round merits there, I wouldn't be without them now.

It was a gloriously fresh gold-and-blue noon, after a steamy night before, when we'd pulled in at the Acapulco bus depot. Perhaps every Mexican trip should start on Saturday night at the Acapulco bus depot, for there is nowhere to go but up. And so we did, to the fourteenth floor of a pleasant hotel.

Our view from the neat balcony, the following Sunday morning, was a full-color page from any resort brochure—a busy tan beach and some bright blue water with a brown man up to his belly in it, cracking mussels on a rock, and some bright glass-bottomed boats tethered and bobbing. Beside the thatched beach umbrellas on the sand were some white bodies, the kind that never make the postcards—people trying to turn into the lean bronzed creatures they felt like inside as they nibbled their potato chips and drank their Cocolocos, for this Sunday's Communion, while little boys scuttled all over, peddling turtles, lizards, sandals, inner tubes. . . .

On another high hotel-room balcony, across from ours, just in front of the great sheltering Carta Blanca Beer sign, which is to Acapulco as the great sheltering Corcovado Christ is to Rio, a blonde woman in a Hawaiian bathing suit was putting her hair up in rollers, while a man in swim trunks beside her thoughtfully scratched his stomach.

And, farther back, on the lush hills, where the hoteltops were ragged with the bony iron skeletons of ten more stories to come, I could virtually count the bolts, as well as—looking down now—the built-in spots on the front seat of the white car we'd just rented and parked across the street. Without those opera glasses I'd never have caught all this splendid local color, or seen a Mexican taxi plunge around the corner to ricochet off our little rented car and keep on going. Though we couldn't do anything about it, still it was nice to know why the rear end dragged.

But back to the fidgety business of packing. Indeed, I was finding it worrisome even to write about, till I finally decided just to travel light and not worry too much.

First, some free-floating general precepts, and then some miscellaneous, related items, each in its own Pliofilm bag.

## GENERAL PRECEPTS

Making a list doesn't solve everything. Still, it is psychologically comforting, rather like putting a paperweight on top of a stack of papers. It gives you the good feeling of having done something forceful, though you haven't, exactly.

The time a list is really essential is when you pack a few days in advance. Then paste on the bathroom mirror a list of what is still to come, if something is. Otherwise your brain can heave a premature sigh of relief and transmute *nearly finished packing* into *finished packing,* and you leave with your walking shoes still under the bed.

And always carry spray cans in the hand luggage. Once I packed a can of hair spray and it oozed all over, so everything smelled like the ladies' room at the Bijou. I haven't felt so discouraged since a pair of blue jeans with the pockets full of dog biscuits got into the washing machine.

If you're flying, pack all the film, exposed or not, in your hand luggage, not in the suitcase, which might get X-rayed. But hand luggage is only magnetically checked. (If you're still doubtful, you can ask for a visual inspection instead.)

Try to avoid getting stuck with a collapsible umbrella. These are still in the experimental stage; you see tourists experimenting with them all the time. It's easier just to come in out of the rain. Also, dodge anything that folds too trickily. Once I took a large tote bag that folded back up into one of its own pockets, like a mother kangaroo trying to get into her own pouch, and it took forty-five minutes.

Tan at home first, if you can, in the swimsuit you'll take. A friend of mine who had been gardening in shorts and shirt went to Saint Kitts with a real gym teacher's tan; neck brown and red to a ·V in the front, arms brown from finger tips to mid-bicep, legs brown from ankles to just above the knee. Her bikini didn't start to cover those vast pale stretches, and she said her bright white feet practically glowed in the dark.

It is easier not to be too particular than it is to pack enough of some favorite brand: to remember that all tobacco has, after all, a tobaccolike effect, all alcoholic beverages get you there sooner or later, all toothpaste spatters the mirror.

According to my husband, a man should have the rear button-down pocket of his traveling trousers deepened enough to accommodate a passport or passport case. (Otherwise, the jacket's inside pocket is the only place it fits, and this is a sports-shirt age.) Any fair-to-middling tailor or seamstress can do it.

Small thank-you gifts are handy. Even though you're not entertained by anyone, there are usually some situations that tips don't quite cover. Regional American things are good, Appalachian things or Indian or Eskimo crafts: little fringy things, fur things, turquoise, silver, dolls. Or small plushy hand towels in trendy colors, or hair ornaments, or cream perfume in little jars, or American-made ballpoint or felt-tip pens.

Some essential paper items are under Notes, page 259, because they would have made this chapter about as long as the trip. Now for several miscellaneous matters:

Some alarm clocks are more dependable than some desk clerks are, and then again, some aren't. Recently, I traveled with an alarm clock that had to be waked up every morning, so that I hardly slept at all, and it didn't seem fair. Be very sure of any travel clock before you buy it.

Airplane sock-slippers are handy, especially for temples in the Orient. Otherwise you get splinters in your feet or holes in your stockings, or have to shuffle along in large ludicrous sacks that won't stay on.

Washcloths aren't standard issue in small foreign hotels, and they're hard to find in Instant Language guides.

Inflatable plastic clothes hangers let drip-dries dry smoother and faster, and most notions departments stock them.

Two clothespins or safety pins make a fair pants hanger or skirt hanger out of a plain wire coat hanger.

Don't throw away a used-up tube of something till you've replaced it. The old wrinkled one is a reminder, and anyway there is usually another squeeze left if you close it in a door hinge.

Instead of nail polish, a nail buffer will keep your nails shiny and presumably healthier. It won't leak, either, and it gives you something constructive to do in airports.

Bath powder travels safest in a fair-size plastic salt shaker with wax paper under the lid, for if it gets loose it can really fog up a wardrobe.

A fine crochet needle is handy for working snagged threads back into knit fabric instead of cutting them off.

A popular bit of folk wisdom says you should cut the leg off a pair of panty hose—the leg with a run in it—and save the rest to wear eventually with a pair whose other leg was amputated for the same reason.

While the theory is good, few women live long enough to find out how it works, because women are either right-legged or left-legged, when it comes to runs. By the time a run is finally achieved in the correct leg, the other pair is long gone. Like finally locating the other mitten.

Panty hose remain the best bet, though, especially under pants, which hide the runs anyway. And pants are all right nearly everywhere now, or, if they aren't, the proprietor lets you know. In San Francisco, recently, a woman wasn't allowed in a restaurant till she took the pants off her pants suit, leaving her in a minimum mini, which the management allowed was quite all right.

Now, about

## HAIR

Natural hair is best to travel in—hair in its own color, straight or curly the way it came, if you can bear it. If not, there is always the intensive-care department of the local hairdresser's, which is usually interesting even if you can't read the movie magazines. But try to remember to bring along a snapshot of yourself with your hair looking the way you like it to look. Then Maestro Luigi or Mr. Richard isn't flying blind.

I've also had good luck with hairdressing instructions translated into the language of the country. Perhaps you can have this done before you go, if you're near a university or a language school. Or do it when you get there; it isn't hard to find an amiable bilingual hotel clerk who'll write it out. (He can also translate any manicuring instructions you might have, and perhaps he'd better. Some manicurists have the spirit of a true surgeon when it comes to the cuticle.)

I like the way my hairdressing instructions look in Polish:

Proszę o pofarbowanie na bronzowo górnej części włosów, lecz o pozostawienie siwych na stronach. Na czole chcę mieć coś w rodzaju grzywki ułożonej w zakręcony lok. Po bokach włosy zaczesane do góry, *nie* powinny się zakręcać wokoło uszu . . .

And they are even more impressive in Japanese, like the declaration for a small war:

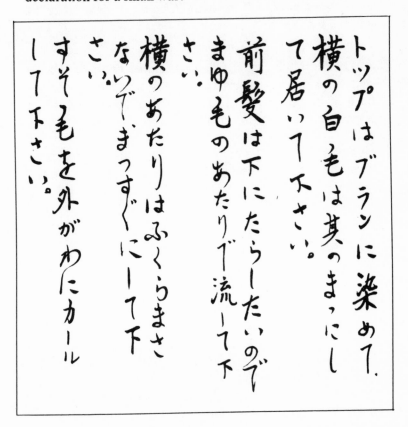

But be sure you can trust your translator. This could have been the long way around for color it pink. (What it says is: "Please put a brown tint on the top of my hair but leave the gray at the sides. I like something of a bang on the forehead, and my hair up on the sides, *not* curling around the ears.")

By the way, the French word for back-combing, or teasing, is *crêpage*. That is the noun. Say: *"On fait le crêpage."* If you want more, tell the man, *"Beaucoup de crêpage."* If not, tell him, *"Pas de crêpage."* If you prefer a sleeker look, then it's *"Pas trop frisé, assez lisse."*

When in doubt, take an item that does two jobs. For instance, a hairbrush makes a good back-scratcher if your sunburn peels, but a Chinese back-scratcher makes a poor hairbrush. So take the hairbrush. Gold bedroom slippers can double for evening slippers, and some nightgowns for evening gowns. (Avoid white nightgowns, which tend to blend with white bedsheets and get left behind.)

And so, finally, to

## CLOTHES

Today's traveling costume seems to be just that. You see some odd things. People used to dress up, especially for airplanes, but now they dress down, so far down it doesn't leave much for buses. You'd probably be all right in what you wore yesterday, if you were up and around, plus a raincoat.

A woman named Name Withheld wrote a fervent letter to one of the big travel guidebooks, saying that for a two- or three-month summer trip she wore what she had on, carrying only a flight bag and a shoulder bag.

"I wear a dark, flared, lined rayon suit, longsleeved, with

a dark lace shell [she wrote]. This becomes an evening gown, train-travel dress, restaurant costume, or sight-seeing outfit, as the occasion demands. I do not take another outfit. . . ." And this apparently works for her, though it reminds me of the combination eggbeater-potscraper-and-applecorer that isn't very good at doing anything.

On the other hand, I'd prefer it to some of the experts' recommended closetfuls—four drip-dry blouses, two sports dresses, two cocktail dresses, and so on, including things I didn't know people still wore, and after you've packed those camisoles, you start in on the thermal underwear.

Then there is the two-or-more-seasons trip. I believe this is a matter for everyone to mess up in his own way. Some have clothes sent on ahead to hotels or good friends there (they must be *very* good friends), and sometimes the clothes don't arrive in time. Some plan to buy what they need when the weather changes, and end up spending three days hunting for something they can stand or that fits. If winter is approaching, some count on long johns and sweaters to add in layers, like the wallpaper in an ancient boardinghouse, and shed when it warms up. This is probably the best, though on a chilly day it makes you look fat, or at any rate fatter.

But, as we have noted, it is a personal matter. What you pack is a compromise, as a rule, between how you want to look and what you want to bother with, just as a woman's figure is generally a compromise between how she wants to look and what she wants to eat. Once you've checked out the weather and packed some cotton for hot places, some wool for cold places, and some handy man-made fibers for the places in between, you take what seems logical or comfortable or good-looking, or all three, if you're lucky.

It seems to me that the main thing is not to take any clothes that are brand-new and totally untried. Even though you take them anyway, it's good to know in advance that they're going to spot easy, wrinkle fast, dry slow, and bag in the seat. Indeed, *everything* should be pretested: flight bags, handbags, make-up, and—as I think I mentioned—books, which may be your only nostrum for the colds in the head and the long, long waits and the occasional fitful flickerings of the *élan vital* that even the blithest traveler can't always avoid.

And, with clothes, something old and dependable is best for other reasons, among them being that having it along is a good excuse to buy something new when you get there. Even if it is so old and easy you can't bear to part with it, that is all right, too.

A neighbor of mine has a friendly old corset like this. The lady, who travels a good deal, is seventy-seven, and her corset as well is getting along in years, to the point where it is no real treat to look at though superbly comfortable.

This poses a problem. She wouldn't be caught dead with it, although—after all—she might have a heart attack during the night, and strangers would be going over her effects, which would be embarrassing. So, every night she parks her corset in the wastebasket, and every morning she puts it back on again.

> *But do not on this noble voyage*
> *Cumber yourself with heavy baggage.*
> —GOETHE'S Faust

> . . . *The only travel tip I ever got was from a sour-faced first class petty officer who told me, the first day I reported aboard: "Walk aft till your hat floats."*
> —DERECK WILLIAMSON

# 10

## Flight #231 Departing at 4:15
## Now Departing at 7:45

*"Tell me again how you and Grandpa came across the plains, Granny!"*

*"Well, dear, we drove to the airport and sat around awhile and then we walked down a long, carpeted, covered tunnel and sat down at the end of it, and pretty soon we were there."*

As I may have indicated earlier, writing a book is rather like packing a suitcase, mainly hindsight and split decisions. There is one other important item you should bring along, and perhaps it should have been tucked into the preceding chapter.

I mean a candy bar. You should pack one immediately into your flight bag, coat pocket, handbag, or bra, though in that case, pack two.

The reason for the candy bar is that in any long or longish journey, there is usually one critical moment when the traveler finds himself starving to death, owing to factors beyond his control, like no food in sight.

What kind of candy bar depends, of course, upon your tastes. Each to his own, though I've noticed that the thin ones tend to crumble, and they melt faster.

Thick is better. My usual choice is Snickers, its only drawback being the name. "I want a Snicker," you tell the man.

"Go right ahead," he answers smartly, or anyway he might. Other than that, a Snicker is a good, all-round, sturdy little candy bar, forthright and full-bodied, yet with a touch of whimsy. Vintage or otherwise, it needs no decanting; just unwrap it and eat it. Then, if you remember to, ask the stewardess why she doesn't have a candy-bar machine up there where she keeps the bum coffee and all the booze.

Indeed, another mystery about airplanes, besides how they stay up there, is why you can't even get a soda cracker or a malted-milk tablet on a nonfood flight, while you can nearly always get a drink. Any passenger can get so thoroughly snockered before he lands, he should get a crack at his oxygen mask before he starts his own glide path down the ramp. Though he probably wouldn't know what to do with it by then. Probably hang it on his ear.

Splashdown. That's when you land.

If you ever noticed, the airplane people keep saying that two drinks do the work of four when you're flying already, but still they keep pushing them. Personally, I always wonder a little when a hostess thinks she has to get her guests that stiff. She must know something about the food that they don't. (I know something about the food, too. When they have any. Don't order the chicken cutlet.)

Maybe there is something the airline doesn't want you to notice? Like the way you bump your shins when you try to cross your legs? Like they're out of towels again in the bathroom? Like the stewardesses aren't as gorgeous as they used to be?

*"What are you so cross about?" Gunther Newton asked curiously, when he had read this far.*

*"I'm not cross," I said. "Really I'm not."*

*But then I thought back. It had been a very cross country trip that I'd just returned from. Everybody was cross, and nothing went the way it does in the airline commercials. The passengers were complaining about the late takeoff, and the stewardess was handing out dirty looks instead of coats, and the pilot sent his dinner back. Maybe he'd ordered the chicken c— Oh, well.*

*Gunther was regarding me with his keen gray eyes. They are the farseeing eyes of a sea captain or an airline passenger accustomed to scanning the closed-circuit TV screen from the tail end of the line, and they can make you uncomfortable.*

*He shook his head slowly.*

*"Are you quite sure it isn't jet lag?" he wanted to know.*

*I shifted uneasily on the camel-saddle stool I usually sit on over at Gunther's. And presently I had to admit it, at least to myself. I was showing some jet-lag symptoms, all right. Once, I saw a little old crippled lady standing outside an airport with her baggage and cane, waiting for the limousine. She nearly missed it, because she was trying so hard to kick a bird. It was a small, blue-chested bird who was just puttering around the sidewalk and hadn't done anything to her that I could see. A clear case of jet lag.*

*"Maybe you're right," I admitted. "But all the same—"*

*"Then perhaps you'd better complain about the jet lag instead of the stewardesses," he suggested. "Or explain about it. And actually, aren't you being a little . . . er . . . feminine about the stews? Maybe they're as cute as they ever were, while on the other hand—" He stopped, with great delicacy. I was sorry I'd brought the matter up.*

Well, about jet lag.

Basically, there are two types. First, there is Outgoing Jet Lag, marked by feeling bad, and thinking sour, and realizing with clarity that your new surroundings don't live up to their advance billing.

Then there is Homecoming Jet Lag, which is similar but more complicated, because of recent culture shock, input overload, feeling broke, and knowing you have to unpack that swollen suitcase, as well as get back into the groove, or the hole. Like having mosquito bites on top of the poison ivy on top of your sunburn; you can't tell one from the other, you only know you itch.

East-West or West-East flights are the worst, because they have you arriving either ahead of your hormones or a respectful distance behind them. North-South flights aren't so bad. As one pilot puts it, they keep your bowels in the same time zone. But the trouble is that there generally aren't as many North-South places you and your bowels want to go as there are East-West places.

Mainly, it seems to be a matter of internal rhythms—more than thirty of them, I understand—which run almost everything. And they are all interdependent, each one fluctuating within a twenty-four cycle, like some giant science-fiction clockworks.

So the airline feeds you before your stomach has pushed the right buttons (those very same buttons you see on the acid-indigestion commercials). But you eat because it's free and it's something to do, while your stomach sits and looks at it.

And when your muscles holler, Exercise! the sign says FASTEN YOUR SEAT BELT. So you try for a nap, abetted by a drink, but it's uneasy sleeping. You can't fool your glands. They knew it wasn't naptime, and they've already produced a good shot of adrenaline, which collides with the bourbon. It's war.

My doctor said you should allow a day for each time zone you go through, for total recovery of all your mental and emotional faculties. He also said all you can do is not eat or drink much before or during a long flight and then take a sleeping pill and go easy the next day, and for this he charged me fifteen dollars.

Yes, and for all this the IATA charges large sums of money. (If you've been living at the bottom of a mine shaft for a while, the IATA is the International Air Transport Association, the association midgets who decide how much room the human knee needs and then squeeze in some more seats and jack up the prices again, for people over sixteen, though they make up for it with low bargain rates every other Thursday that doesn't have an *r* in it.)

—Jack the prices *way* up, I mean. Especially flying over the ocean first class. That's three hundred dollars *extra!* Per person!

Imagine! Three hundred dollars extra so that you can cross your legs and sit with the Beautiful People and get stoned in style! Well, it's lovely up there, and my husband and I always prefer to go first class on overseas flights because of the leg room, though we always go coach because of the three hundred dollars. With my three hundred I could buy a fancy dress and a coat, too. With his three hundred he could buy himself some mink-lined shorts if they happened to tickle his fancy, and I guess they would.

As I say, the IATA tries to keep the prices up, while the passenger tries to keep the dinner down—

*"There you go again," Gunther interrupted. "Maybe you'd better go to bed and take another run at your airplane chapter tomorrow."*

*"You mean I'm still sounding that way?" I asked, in some surprise. Sometimes you can't hear yourself accurately through the buzz of an electric typewriter, and I think my ears were still bothering me a little anyway. "Aerotitis," the doctors call it now, the miserable rotten earache you can get sometimes from flying too high too fast.*

*Gunther nodded, regretfully. "You certainly are," he said. "And I really don't understand all this about the food. Didn't I hear you say once that you thought most planeloads were eating 50 per cent better than they'd have been eating at home? Including you?"*

*I avoided his eyes. Deliver me from a friend with a good memory.*

*"And"—he pressed the point home—"didn't you say you wished you had the recipe for TWA's chocolate mousse, and American's smoked pork with sauerkraut?"*

*"It was the other way around," I said. "But there's still the money."*

*Thoughtfully, Gunther knocked the dottle out of a classy brierwood pipe he'd picked up somewhere off Piccadilly.*

*"Yes, there's the money," he mused. "The expense. Granted, it's a little bit much. But—"*

*"Little bit!" I said.*

*"But didn't you figure out that the train cross-country in a sleeper would cost you 25 per cent more than the plane, with your meals and tips? If you could find the train."*

*"Well, sure," I said. "But two wrongs—"*

*"You don't actually have to fly, you know," he continued reasonably. "Lots of people don't. If you don't have the jelly beans, stay out of the playpen. Or fly standby. Or take a charter. Lots of good cheap charters. Or drive. Take a bus. Take a boat."*

*"Well, yes," I said. "That's so."*

*"And didn't you say once that there's no feeling quite like the feeling once you've fastened your seat belt and dozed off like everybody else while they demonstrate what to do in the unlikely-event-that-additional-oxygen-should-become necessary, and then—"*

*"Yes," I said eagerly. "And nobody would know what to do, either, in the unlikely-event-that-additional-oxygen-*

*should-become-necessary except that one little old lady who really listened because this is her first plane trip."*

*"Okay, so you'd ask her," said Gunther, who wasn't to be deflected. "And you also said that when you finally surge down the runway and angle up with a good jet scream into the wild blue—"*

*"All right, Gunther," I said. "All right."*

And so I will put the rest of my airline information under Notes, at the back of the book, because no matter how I put it down, it seems to sound a little shrewish. Perhaps it won't be so noticeable back there.

As for this part, I'll only add a brief word, a rueful admission that Gunther is right. For I think there is no moment quite like that moment when you are thoroughly aloft, en route and encapsulated, between telephones and mailboxes, far above the once large and now minuscule matters you left behind, diminishing even the streaming prairies and the speedways down there under the celestial honey-and-whipped-cream meadow outside the window as you streak splendidly along toward a not too unpleasant destination, or even a glorious one, and I wish I were on Flight #231 right now and that I had never checked this chapter in with Gunther Newton. He's such a nit-picker.

> *While traveling*
> *I am all free from care*
> *No man knows me;*
> *No man betrays me there.*
> —WATANABE KOHAN

# 11

---

# Will You Remember Me?

*The Greek clergyman asked J. A. and his sister to tea and when they departed, accompanied them back to their hotel repeating, "You will remember me?" "Yes, certainly," said J. A. The clergyman repeated his touching request about fifteen times and each time J. A. (though somewhat surprised) assured him with increasing warmth that he would never forget him. It was only afterwards that they realized that the reverend gentleman was asking for a tip.* —C. S. LEWIS

Once upon a good while ago, when trains ran smoothly and everywhere, a traveling man inquired of the Pullman porter, as the Luxury Limited pulled into New York, "What would you say is the usual tip for this run?"

"Five dollars is about the usual, suh," replied the porter (as I say, this was a good while ago, when there were Pullman porters and they were supposed to talk this way). And so the gentleman gave him five dollars.

"Thank you, suh," the porter said. "And may I say, suh, that you is the first gentleman that ever tipped me the usual."

—Which illustrates clearly a truth about tipping: so few people tell it. When the matter is under discussion, it so often seems necessary to shade the facts for one reason or another, although when the tipper is talking, and not the tippee, he tends to lie downward in the direction of courage, rather than up. And understandably; for often, if the precise truth were known, the tipper would look weak in the head.

For reasons that escape me now, my husband and I recently thought it a good idea to visit the fairy-tale* kingdom of Monaco, which is eight sunny hilly square miles packed with twenty-three thousand happy smiling people, each with one hand out and the other one already in your pocket.

We stayed a night amid the somewhat seedy splendors of the Metropole, and the next morning, while my husband bailed us out downstairs, I left the equivalent of a U.S. dollar on the dresser for the maid, then waited for the baggage boy.

(This brings up a good point, by the way: why tip the maid after a one-night stand? Unless she performed some specific service for you, all she did was clean up after the last roomer, and it's like tipping the dishwasher for the clean plates your dinner arrives on. But you expected it to arrive on clean plates; that's part of the price of a restaurant meal, just as your hotel bill is supposed to include the price of a freshly made bed. However, many things in this world don't make any sense, and the general rule is still one dollar per night in a good hotel, fifty cents in a more modest establishment.)

And so the baggage boy eventually came, mustachioed, blue-smocked, fifty years old if he was a day. He trotted briskly over to the dresser, where he scooped the francs up and into his pocket.

So I put down some more for the maid and followed the blue smock downstairs and outside. There he stowed the bags in our car and turned to me expectantly.

---

* Fairy-tale is the mandatory adjective for Monaco, though pippy-poo will do nicely.

"But you already have yours," I said, in impeccable French, and climbed into the car and shut the door.

And every word of that is true except for the last nineteen. Actually, in moments of stress my French becomes so peccable it isn't much good. Moreover, I proved myself a sniveling coward. The shabby truth is that I tipped the oaf again.

What was I afraid of? That he would discover I wasn't Princess Grace after all? I think he knew that already. Did I think we'd meet again someday? Not on your tintype; not if I saw him first. Was I afraid he would hit me? Not really; anyway, my husband was bigger than he was. Or was I at all costs avoiding a dirty look, overt evidence that someone didn't love me (even though I didn't love him)? This is probably closer to the mark, or to the shilling or the franc or whatever currency we're dealing with.

Well, I was rattled, I tell myself. And it was another country. And it's easier to be brave in your own language. . . .

A man I know gave a business dinner in the private dining room of a large San Francisco hotel. He ordered the seven-fifty *table d'hôte* all around. With cocktails and wine it came to twelve dollars per place, or one hundred and eighty dollars for the fifteen people. Service was mediocre, and they'd substituted creamed canned peas for the fresh asparagus he had ordered to accompany the chops. (I was there, which is how I know.)

Even so, my friend tipped twenty dollars, and he was surprised that the waiter just stood there. "I'm sorry, sir," he said with an ingratiating smile, "but we get 15 per cent."

My friend considered this, with rather a pensive air. "As you know," he said, "this is a voluntary act on my part. And you say it isn't enough?"

Big beam. "No," said the waiter.

"I'm sorry, too," my friend said, and he pocketed the twenty, and left.

It is customary to say that everyone hates tipping—the tipper because it is an expensive nuisance, the tippee because it lessens his dignity. But I wish I could find more waiters and bellhops who feel that way. In fact, I haven't met any yet. All the help I run into seem to like the system a lot, and the bigger the tip is, the better they seem to like it.

I've noticed, too, that the talented ones apply so much ingenuity to insuring large and frequent tips that considerable professional pride must be involved, after all. It is not the waiters, it is the customers who start antitipping crusades, who leave printed cards that say "Thank you for your excellent service; I don't approve of tipping but I will remember you in my prayers," and who probably get mugged in the alley.

Not even all customers are against tipping, either. Some like it because it makes them feel better, in some obscure way. Some enjoy being Charlie-off-the-yacht, especially on an expense account. Some simply enjoy the good feeling they get from dispensing careful sums to their inferiors (or to the people they'd like to consider so).

Thus, like the sadist who marries the masochist, there is often something in it for both parties, which is probably why the tipping system is still around. Anything that we honestly want to get rid of, we generally manage to, like corsets or the bubonic plague or the tsar.

And so the small war continues, each side developing its own weapons. The bellhop can take three trips and tips to deliver what deserved only one, and the customer can say on arrival, "I'll take care of you when I leave," and then somehow forget to. The cabdriver can extract his tip before he returns the change, and the passenger can leave the door swinging wide in heavy traffic. Or if the dining-room steward is cross and lazy, the traveler can tip him half the total due him midway in the cruise and at the end of it give him a sealed thank-you, in one of those envelopes packed in chapter ten or possibly lifted from the ship's writing room.

*When a difficult guest tips a bellman poorly, it is customary to return his car to the parking lot with emergency brake on, while traveling steadily forward at 30 m.p.h. all the way.*
　　　　　　　　—JOHN BRADY, former bellhop

*While manning the service-desk phones, I took a call from a guest who had checked out and traveled halfway home before remembering several suits in his room's closet. I checked the room, found the suits, wrapped, insured, and mailed them to him that night. He said he would take good care of me, but I never heard from him again. Postage alone was $3.85.*   —Ibid.

And yet, somewhere on the battlefield one must plant one's flag. Myself, I think a tip is still basically a monetary thank-you above and beyond the call of etiquette for an extra service or a standard job done as politely and good-naturedly and well as the person can do it, and I try to act accordingly, except when scared.

It's true that this whole sizable slippery subject is further complicated by the customs and currencies of different countries plus assorted diddlypoopery, including percentages, attitudes, and situations. Most travel books try to move this

tips, on the theory that charity should begin at home. They just linger a minute after he stands up. On the other hand, some women have been known to leave an additional tip on the sly to make up for an embarrassingly stingy one.

The worst tippers are:
> baseball players
> dentists
> doctors
> lawyers
> Argentine tourists.

Priests are nearly always excellent tippers.

You needn't tip the doorman of an apartment when you visit a friend there. Your friend's punctual and handsome handouts are supposed to have covered these things, no matter what the doorman thinks.

And you needn't tip people for doing what you didn't hire them to do, like guarding hubcaps, any more than you must pay for the pink plastic God-bless-our-home plaques that worthy charities send you, all unasked for, in the mail. In foreign places you can pretend cordial stupidity. Just hearty beaming thanks.

And you still don't tip:
> anyone who's done nothing at all for you
> anyone you see socially, or might
> proprietors of any U.S. shop
> customs officials
> immigration officials
> pursers on boats
> ships' officers
> Boy Scouts
> Girl Guides
> desk clerks
> people in Tahiti.

And of course, airline personnel, which includes the curb-side check-in men. They, too, are airline personnel, though they never remembered to tell me this when I tipped them, as I did for years.

At a resort, you might ask if it is a union or a nonunion place. If it is nonunion, the bellhop's pay is about twenty-five dollars a week. Tips are probably the reason he took the job.

In a resort where you stay longer than a day, news of your tipping habits (or any other interesting ones) travels fast. That is because hotel resorts are so often family-run: the bartender's wife runs the gift shop, her son by a former marriage waits table poolside when he isn't parking cars, the bell captain is his brother-in-law. . . .

What is overtipping in Cultural Lag, Wyoming is under-tipping in Manhattan. In plushy restaurants there, the rate is 20 per cent.

Elsewhere, like Europe, when a 15 per cent service charge is included in the restaurant check, you leave a little extra —from 3 per cent to 5 per cent.

Overtipping never makes anyone love you, though it makes some people pretend to, which can be better than nothing.

Overtipping for ordinary services already received makes no sense unless the help is giving you the deep freeze and you are stuck in the place for several more days.

When to overtip:

1. As a reward for returning something valuable, like your passport or your money or your baby. Honesty is apt to flourish more hardily if it isn't always its own reward, so let's encourage it as much as we can.

2. As payment for doing an unpleasant job you would

otherwise have had to do yourself, like hauling a sixty-six-pound suitcase two blocks through a blizzard.

3. As a bribe—to the *maitre d'* for a decent restaurant table or to the doorman for a taxi at 6:00 P.M.

*It is impossible to overtip* the maitre d'.  —GAEL GREENE

"Please don't overtip," said my guest, a knowledgeable Frenchwoman. "It makes it so hard on us. And this is a terribly expensive place."

She wasn't just whistling the *Marseillaise*. We were in Paris, at a Michelin two-star restaurant with delusions of Maxim's.

The lunch was quite good. Tender artichoke bottoms, at about a dollar a bottom, and turbot soufflé—they must have flown the little fellow over first class from New Orleans before they souffléd him—and a bottle of Pouilly-Fuissé they weren't giving away that day, and a dessert I can't remember. But I remember the check. You'd have thought they'd cooked us the national bird.

I paid it, and, *le service* being *compris,* left only a modest heap of additional francs, say about the size of a young truffle.

But I am an American, and of course the waiters knew it. They had been infinitely solicitous, expecting *le bon Dieu* knows what largesse, and when they saw they weren't going to get it, I thought they would spit in my eye. So I sidled out, afraid to turn my back—I didn't want it spat upon, either—and never returned, though I would rather have liked to in spite of the prices. The restaurant was handily located next door to my hotel, and the chef certainly knew his way around a kitchen.

And so, not overtipping may make it easier on the citizens of the country you're visiting, while it makes it a little sticky for you. What the moral to all this is, I haven't the slightest idea.

But in these difficult situations, I often think of my good friend Wally Frederick. After hosting a *service-compris* luncheon for thirty at the Tour d'Argent, he walked out between two rows of beaming, bowing waiters, beaming right back as he shook each and every one of them by the hand.

PART THREE

# Eating My Words

# 12

---

# Terrine Terrain:
# Where Pop Does the Cooking

*. . . I have noticed that it's customary with most
cookbook writers to throw in an occasional well-
traveled paragraph, to indicate that they haven't
spent their lives huddled over their own kitchen
ranges. "I first tasted this dish at Maxim's," they'll
write. "And how I wished I could hide like a little
mouse in the corner of that famous kitchen and see
exactly what went into that famous sauce. . . ."*
                                    —The I Hate to Cook Book

He was a solid, commanding figure behind the cooking
counter in the small room, tall in his chef's hat, which made
him taller than he was. But there was no doubt of his solid-
ity. Portly. Three pounds this side of fat. (Never trust a
skinny chef.)

What torrents of béarnaise, I thought, what foothills of
*foie gras* and the best sweet butter must have gone into the
ponderous parabola that zoomed gently from under his second chin and, with growing exuberance, out and over and
smoothly down to approximately the sixth button of the
white work coat. It kept him erect, his front did, and when
he leaned over to stress a point, he bent stiffly from the hips,
like a symphony conductor in a cardboard shirt.

His chef's bonnet was skinny. It didn't balloon like the

hats on the chefs who flip pancakes in store windows. Skinny and straight, like a white paper sack. Under it, the ruddy face was lined—he was in his sixties—and the nose was masterful, the eyes sharp. Behind him stood the assistant, built like a linebacker for the Los Angeles Rams. Observant, and one felt that he'd better be.

But the focus was on the *chef-professeur* himself, Charles Narsès, as he worked.

He worked hard. Outdoors on the shabby side street, Paris went about her midafternoon business all in the drizzly day; but indoors, he worked, with intensity and a blunt economy of movement. Chopped the carrot, carved the mushroom, shook the pan, *so*—definitively, that was the word— to his own obbligato of fast French.

Behind him hung the copper saucepans, bottoms and sides heat-smudged, needing a polish. Working saucepans, not decorative touches. In front of him was a minimal expanse of bare wood surface, a small cooking range, and a sink, with one large gray square-shouldered sponge in evidence. A believable kitchen.

In front of that, facing him, attentive in our school chairs equipped with writing arms, were we students. For I was among them, a mouse in the corner. What had brought me to this?

As in so many areas, the question is easier than the answer. I could say that I came in to get out of the rain. But that really wouldn't be so. There are other, more probable places. Moreover, one cannot sit at the feet of the Master on a drop-in basis; one makes arrangements in advance. And in French.

Or I could say I was tired of knowing so little about a subject that has always interested me, mildly. But that wouldn't be quite accurate, either. I've found that ignorance has its advantages. You don't expect much of yourself, and it is more comfortable that way.

Well, a cat can look at a king, if she pays admission. Mainly, I was there because it had seemed about time, to me, to get down to some hard-core fancy eating. But first, I wanted to see a little of what went into it behind the scenes.

After all, my liver and I had been through a good deal together—through a couple of decades of fast-cooked meals, with a considerable assist from the canned, the frozen, and the ready-mixed. Although I would have backed my liver any day against the *chef-professeur*'s, the fact remained that I had been wading in the culinary tide pools. And now it might be refreshing, I thought, to take a short swim in the walloping ocean of *haute cuisine*. Or—to change the metaphor without drying off—if *la haute cuisine* may be viewed as a river rising in France with distributaries flowing out of it, I had been living for years at the far tail end of one of them, up the crick.

It is true that I had eaten French, on occasion—in France, and here and there, some good places, some bad places. I had even sent the wine back once. But that was in Sausalito. Anybody can send the wine back in Sausalito. I thought, now, that it would be instructive to go straight to the source.

Accordingly, my husband and I had made reservations for the following week at two of the eleven Michelin three-star* shrines along the gourmet trail, though not both on the same day, *Mon Dieu!* One was La Pyramide, in Vienne, three stars for food and four for ambience. The other was L'Ous-

---

* Three Michelin stars mean "one of the best tables in France, well worth the journey." Two stars mean "excellent cuisine, worth a detour." One star means "a good restaurant in its class." Michelin's crossed fork-and-spoon is an equally instructive hieroglyph referring to ambience, luxury, and comfort, ranging from one to five. Restaurants aplenty earn forks and spoons, but Michelin is miserly with stars.

tau de la Baumanière in Les Baux, a three-star five fork-and-spoon, impressive as any five-star general. Each has been called by its devotees the World's Best Restaurant.

—As have a great many other places. Surely this is as subjective a concept as Miss America in these rarefied realms where the only absolute is faultless classic cookery.* For if the cooking ceased to be faultless—if, say, a middle-aged carrot crept into the soup—it would be like the Miss America contender showing up knock-kneed or squinting. No ball game.

But as it is, given certain specific excellences, much depends on whether the Miss America contest judges prefer blondes to brunettes, or short girls to tall girls, or a harmonica solo to Joyce Kilmer's "Trees" done with gestures. Or, on the restaurant front, whether one prefers simplicity to formality, bustle to quiet, the Lyonnaise accent to the Provençal, or whether—basically and deep down—one really wants the lo-cal broiled beef patty and hold the fries.

At any rate, we knew that calling Pyramide or Baumanière a good restaurant was like calling Escoffier a good cook. And we had nothing to lose but our francs, our waistlines having been long since abandoned somewhere in Brittany, along with a tall stack of lobster shells, fruit pits, and bottles that once held good dark wine. In a counterclockwise drive from Paris to Paris, the previous few weeks, we had tunneled with our teeth through Normandy, Brittany, and the realm of the fat, crackling Périgord goose. We had tasted of the creamy Reblochon and the Roquefort and the chèvre, and the thick Breton pancakes and the thin Breton crêpes, the salt-grazed mutton, the truffles and the good fat liver, and the sole and the *raie* and the shrimp, and

* "Establishing a recipe," says Raymond Oliver, another three-star restaurateur, "involves repeating, from memory, an identical gesture in identical circumstances. It is a symbolic act."

the starfish and the garfish, and the crab and the dab, and the plaice and the dace, and the skate and his mate, and the mackerel and the pickerel, and the really truly twirly-whirly eel. . . .

But these two immense three-star hurdles remained ahead. And that is why, O Best Beloved, it seemed a reasonable move to check in first at Le Cordon Bleu, École de Cuisine, and learn a little of what went on in a classic kitchen.

It was a brave decision for me to make. As I have mentioned earlier, I don't really speak the language. Indeed, I don't even speak it in English; for it seems to be an extremely elegant *in*-language all its own that the gourmet writers have developed, a nearly indigestible language, rich with the velvet density of a fine pâté. Nor is it given to all of us to understand it, let alone speak it.

The imperative nudge of the garlic, they say. Or the suavely understated *beurre blanc*. Or the peremptory chic of the unadorned terrine. And some of these migratory full-bodied gourmets get to breathing so hard you have to check back to make sure they're still writing about food. As one wrote, in a discussion of the *antipasto* at a high-priced San Francisco beanery, "Prosciutto, that virile ham of Italy, is a willing groom, ready to be married off to a bevy of sweet lovelies, able to live happily ever after with sugar-sweet melon, ripe pears, or with about-to-burst-from-sweetness figs . . ."—which seems to me to be carrying free speech pretty far.

Too, it took financial courage for me to enroll at Le Cordon Bleu. The six-week demicourse costs a cool two thousand francs (about four hundred American dollars). That is for the pleasure of cooking two mornings a week and watching the *chef-professeur* cook all five afternoons. If you've paid attention, this earns you a *Certificat Élémentaire,* which might get you a job back home washing dishes at Chock Full O'Nuts. But if you spend a year and sixteen thousand francs, and finally pass your *truite en gelée,* your *chaud-froid de volaille,* and your *crêpes Grand Marnier,* you are graduated with the impressive *Grand Diplôme.*

I figured that one twenty-five-franc afternoon would be about right. Even so, that was five dollars, which can still buy you a merry afternoon in Paris. Eat waffles in the Rue de la Gaité, whoop around the Métro, go stare at the Lady and the Unicorn at the Cluny. Or window-shop the Limoges and the practical-joke place on the Rue de Paradis. Or take the *bateau mouche* down the Seine, or sit around Le Dôme and wonder where the intellectuals went, or is that the way they look now. Or make a down payment on some acupuncture at the clinic on the Rue Danton. Or buy a lovely chocolate Eiffel Tower, or five strawberries the size of golf balls at Fauchon . . . And I had certainly considered all these things before biting the bullet, before I finally checked in at the modest store turned school that afternoon, along with a couple of dozen more dedicated students from half a dozen countries, including China. And here we sat, now, in three intent rows.

On my right was a pretty Danish girl named Marina, who spoke some English. She was the new second wife of an aging American author who evidently wished she could cook, too. On my left was Fred, a serious blond lad from Michigan who was going the whole thirty-two-hundred-dollar route, with an eventual eye on the kitchen of the Pontchartrain Hotel back in Detroit.

The demonstration began. M. Narsès washed his hands and wiped them on a clean old-fashioned roller towel. He surveyed, briefly, the vegetables in front of him: a tomato, a potato, two carrots, some assorted greenery. Then he produced from under the counter a fair-size fish. Then some eggs.

Right here my problems started. This man was going to cook three things at once. The serious lad whispered to me, "You're lucky. Some days it's four."

Cooking one thing at once is enough for me. Even watching one thing at once. So at this point I must resort briefly to my notes:

Salts water in big pot. Demonstrates *mire-poix,* chops fast, just like J. Child. Wonder if knows J. C. Chops all veg. Mentions *oseille.* What is? Can't remember. Ask Fred. "Shhh." Must look up.

Dumps in veg., dram. moment. *"Frais,"* he says sternly. Sev. times. *"Frais."* Shakes soup pot. *Vigoureusement.* Lets simmer.

Fish dish. *Bonne femme?* Mushrms & garlic. 200 grams fish per person. "Cod," Fred whispers. Sharp knife. Digs small bloody thing out of fish. Hands fish to Asst. to wash, squeeze. Chops garlic fine. Exactly like J. C.

Gets out old sieve, mashes veg. *Où est le blender?* Ask Fred, F. shrugs, mutters "Wait till you see him whip eggwhites, wears your arm out." Adds, "But it's the *only* way." Agree. Yes *sir.*

Reheats purée. Adds *crème de riz.* Where get c. de r. at home? Dollop sour cream. Pours into hot broth. No, hot broth into c. de r., then cream. Prob. important, what add to what.

Back to fish. Big lump butter, iron pan, adds garlic. Big brown mushrooms. Slices some, carves some, twirls and carves simult., stunning shape like small factory ventilator.

Stirs soup, finds coarse salt, rattles it into fish pan. Pulls off soup, sprinkles flour on pot lid. Why? Cuts spuds long-wise, puts cod & spuds in skillet.

Oh, the pace was quickening now, fast and furious. No dawdling, no staring at the sink. All at once he had six hands for mashing butter into powdered sugar, pouring *vin blanc sec* onto the fish, chopping more *oseille,* must be good stuff, that *oseille.* And I lost track of which dish was which, for wondering if his head didn't get awfully hot under that hat and enjoying the good smells. Really burgeoning now. Lovely.

O boy. Big jug, Grand Marnier. Big orange. Scrapes for zest of orange. Lightly. (*"Légèrement! Légère-ment!"*) No white part.

Washes hands. Square yellow laundry soap, no hand lotion. Separates 3 eggs. (Marina whispers, "Always beat by hand." Okay, okay.)

Beats yolks. Adds 25 gr. flour, hot milk, beats like hell. Thick paste. Thins it. Asst. standing by like surg. nurse. ("Scalpel! Spatula! Whisk!") Asst. hands over *vanille* & pink coloring. Chef beats eggw. a minute. Then Asst. beats & beats & beats. Finally chef pours pale pink foam into soufflé dish, scrapes it off even, heats tray in oven. One minute. Puts in soufflé. Slams oven door. I jump a foot. "Doesn't matter," Fred says. "It'll hold for an hour, even out of the oven. It's all that beating." So M. Narsès said, giving door another resounding slam: *"Une heure entière. . . ."*

He made *crème printanière, cabillaud Bercy,* and *soufflé au Grand Marnier, Mercredi* 28 *Avril.* 1430.

Well, everything turned out fine, and three students bought the three dishes. That is what Le Cordon Bleu does —sells them to someone for a late lunch or an early dinner. Business is business.

Leaving, I remembered to ask Fred why the professor

sprinkled the flour on the soup-pot lid. He explained promptly that this meant *hot,* to remind bystanders not to seize the pot lid. A sound idea, I thought, and worth remembering, though it would have been even more sensible to buy some new pot lids. My copper-bottomed pots at home have black plastic lid knobs that don't get hot, even though the pot does. I thought of telling M. Narsès about them, but then I changed my mind. His aspect was forbidding now. He looked tired, too, and no wonder. All that cooking, five days a week, every week of the world—

One thing I've noticed about famous restaurants is that the people who live near them don't eat there; they eat somewhere else. It is the rest of the world that beats a path to the celebrated door, I was thinking on the following Wednesday morning, as we followed the clearly marked road to L'Oustau de la Baumanière.

Of course, there are good reasons. For one, there is the familiarity that breeds boredom, if not contempt, with restaurants as with anything else, from shops to sights. One values his own discoveries—as we noted earlier—more than the landmarks.

Too, celebrated restaurants so often prove the truth of the old definition that a celebrity is someone who no longer does the things that made him a celebrity. Smothered by its laurels as the corned beef by the cabbage, a restaurant can stop paying attention to anything but its press notices. Some margarine can ooze into the butter, some milk into the ice cream. As Chef Hans Kalitzki has remarked, "Sometimes you can substitute black olives for truffles. People don't really know the difference."

Not long before we left for France, we had dined at the French restaurant currently known as San Francisco's best. If I had cooked the dinner myself, I would have considered it highly creditable—the *quenelles* light as marshmallows, the fish delicate and good, though I'd have thrown out the spinach-soufflé recipe the same night. And *les pêches,* though they flamed, were canned. It wasn't quite worth the fifty-three dollars for two with a half-bottle of all-right wine, exclusive of tip. Worse, the decibels bounced like Ping-pong balls off the low ceiling. And worst of all, other customers were visibly waiting to take our expensive places, so that we felt compelled to eat and run.

But that was San Francisco, and this was France. This was terrine terrain, the land of a thousand sauces, where food is not only big business but an art form, *controlée* like the French wines, and where—only recently—a contender was eliminated in a search for the best *ouvrier de cuisine* because he added onion to his chicken Marengo. For rules are rules, and though a little informality seems to be creeping in now—even some rarefied restaurants listing some down-to-earth dishes like the *choucroute,* the *pot-au-feu,* the lamb stew—the three-star accent is still on the classic *grande cuisine,* things *pâté*d, *foie*d, brandied, and sauced to a resounding fare-thee-well, stuffed with the chopped liver and lights from the fattest *poule de Bresse,* and beaten. For hours. By hand.

That morning, driving with my husband through the tawny, craggy, increasingly desolate Provence countryside to Les Baux, I own to some truculent thoughts. It might have been partly the *petit mistral* that was ripping around Arles when we left it—Van Gogh's angry, nervous, ceaseless wind that churns the wheatfields to roiling amber and the hair to a crow's nest. But I know it was my insecurities, too, popping like measles. This can happen, sometimes, to an American in France.

The day before, though we'd had no trouble making a reservation at Baumanière by long-distance phone, I knew that we might have had, for some of the better French restaurants have a quota on Americans. Otherwise—as the owner of Grand Vefour in Paris explained it—his regulars would be disturbed. "If there are too many Americans they will believe themselves in a tourist restaurant," he said, "as happens with Tour d'Argent."

I suppose this is understandable. We are so many, and we therefore loom larger and louder (though I understand from the Germans that nothing outboors the German tourist, and the Japanese equally deplore the Japanese, and the Swedes the Swedes). We blush for our countrymen as we do for our families.

I remember an American couple across the dining room one day at an inn in Noves. They ordered two tumblers of straight gin, added their own vermouth from a bottle they carried, then complained loudly that they couldn't read the menu and they didn't want that much food anyway. Madame appeared promptly, to assure them in cold, polite, precise English that they could order exactly what they wanted: as much or as little.

And so one is aware of these things.

On the other hand, these are exceptions now, it seems to me, not the rule. Few of us are that thickheaded, and many Americans know a great deal about food—enough to surprise Madame, as well as the French author of a glossary written for the French that I saw at a Paris kiosk. Among the entries was "American Cuisine: We've got some leftovers that we can hash up, some cold spaghetti, some weak coffee, and we serve ketchup." And California decor, it continued, means: "We've got plastic tables, plastic chairs, plastic dishes, and the headwaiter wears blue jeans."

———

Well, *chacun à son goo,* as the Yankee said, throwing his plate of *tripes à la mode de Caen* into the Seine. There are some things the French don't know beans about, either.

Salad. They can't make a green salad that California wouldn't blush over. Crackers. They need biscuit lessons from Peek Frean or Huntley & Palmer or Nabisco. Bread. French bread isn't in it with the German, and French *croissants* are generally as light and flaky as a week-old bagel. (There's a vault where they age them, under the Louvre.)

And their pastry is a far, damp cry from the Danish, the English, the Swedish, the Viennese. And they can't be especially sound on fruit or they could never have come up with such a gross miscalculation as their *poire Belle Hélène,* unless they simply didn't like Hélène.

Moreover, the French may have the world's tidiest bottoms, but they also have the world's steamiest armpits. When our waiter at Rocamadour reached far over us to serve the rich roast goose, it was a violent olfactory confrontation, and the goose lost.

Yes, and coffee! Brillat-Savarin said dessert without cheese is a one-eyed beauty (which he stole from Confucius, who say a meal without rice is a one-eyed beauty) and I say dessert without coffee is a one-eyed beauty, but in France, try to get the two at once. The waiter looks at you kindly, the way the sanitarium nurse regards Teddy Roosevelt about to charge up San Juan Hill again. But the coffee never comes, and it has you pondering the marvelous illogicality of the logical French, who will defend to the death their right to do as they please but won't let other people do as they please unless they happen to please their way.

But on to the restaurant before the lunch gets cold. At this very moment, surely, they were holding services for the baby lamb untimely torn from his mother before they laid him out *en croute.*

It was a lovely bright noonday at Les Baux. We stopped first to explore the tumbled ruin of the Dead City, a skein of tangled streets twisting up and up to jagged castle parapets at the top. Far below in the valley, we could see the tranquil inn. The Dead City is tranquil now, too, and quiet, except for the tinkle of several cash registers; but back in the 1400's it must have been harsh with the screams of the peasants the old viscount used to throw over the side for fun. And the summer evenings surely shimmered and bubbled with the music of the troubadours assembled for the old Court of Love, which was apparently a mock-up for the Woodstock Festival.

It was on the sun-dappled lawn of L'Oustau de la Baumanière a little later, sipping a vermouth cassis in the glow of the blazing geraniums beside the turquoise pool as I tried to decide between the *bisque de homard* and the *mousse de grives,* that I realized this was the life I was born for. I wondered about the probable sins in a former lifetime that have me muddling about in my own kitchen now. But my husband suggested it was perhaps the other way around—perhaps a matter of getting the KP over in this incarnation and storing up credit for the next. A comforting hypothesis, at any rate . . . And presently, behind us, we heard the waiter's murmured *"S'il vous plaît, m'sieur, 'dame"* and followed him into the vaulted dining room, like a low-slung cathedral, the sunlight filtered by the willows outside.

Our table was beside the fireplace. No fire in it, but nearby, standing tall on a sideboard with a commanding view of the room, was a great vase of shaggy, half-wilted dahlias. Not quite to the heads-hanging-over-the-lifeboat stage, certainly not dead yet. Just terribly, terribly tired.

-----

It was a lovely lunch.

First, a *mousse de grives,* though I wouldn't have ordered it if I had remembered in time that *grives* are thrushes. I would rather not eat something that sings (although I don't mind eating something that moos). But the French don't feel that way. Indeed, if you're a French bird, you haven't much of a choice. Either you're some frowsty old lady's *bébé,* kept jailed in a cage, or you're mashed into a mousse, and that's *it.* But the mousse was delicate and perfect, and it was touchingly shaped like a clutch of eggs.

The lamb, too, had me thinking some poignant thoughts. It was undoubtedly a premature delivery, and the tender baby-pink meat came to the table swaddled in flaky bunting.

But—here was a surprise—not a thing came with it. Not one tiny carrot or scrap of parsley, only the bare meat on a bare plate. This was a *gaffe* on our part, we realized. We should have ordered something else. A bean or two, or a potato puff, or perhaps some little fish thing. Like the *bouquet de crevettes* at a neighboring table, lovely as a prom corsage, the shrimps' delicate antennae bunched for a rosy, feathery, frothy look, the beady eyes looking surprised.

And yet, you would expect some little garnish for the lamb, considering the price of it. As my husband pointed out, they could have included a lambskin coat. But then again, as *I* pointed out, this wasn't the businessman's special at the Elks' Club. This was *à la carte* at Baumanière. If they'd meant lamb and beans, they'd have said lamb and beans. The French are very precise that way.

Well, you don't go to France to eat vitamins. If they didn't care, we didn't care. We had our bottle of Châteauneuf-du-Pape to keep us warm, and a witty little wine it was, virtually a laff a minute. And as it turned out, we wouldn't have had room for even a sprig of parsley, because of the confections that lay ahead.

"What should we do besides skip lunch?" I asked again.

"Maybe rent a dog for the evening?" my husband suggested. To clean our plates, we occasionally enlist the aid of our Saint Bernard at home, and unfortunately that was where he was.

So I did what any other woman would do under the circumstances: unpacked, shook out, and hung up the long gold jersey dress I was going to wear, wondered if it was all right, decided it was, decided it wasn't, unpacked another, decided the first was better after all, and then we set out for a good rousing walk around the town.

Vienne didn't seem much of a town, as French towns go, and, under a particularly somber sky that day, the Roman ruins looked more ruined than most. We saw the sawed-off pyramid itself, rather a chummy little pyramid, no higher than a barn door (I think it probably shrinks in memory as the dinner expands), and we saw the scruffy town market, looking like the refrigerator vegetable compartment when you've been away for a while. I hoped they'd done their marketing early, as we strolled past the restaurant on the side street renamed Boulevard Fernand Point.

It was an ample two-story place, like a comfortable French country house—green lawn, red geraniums, all squarely walled in—across the street from a shatteringly noisy discothèque, hordes of long-haired bell-bottomed kids pouring out and in. I pondered their idiocy in spending a Sunday afternoon and undoubtedly a franc or two in that dark cave, when they could be saving their strength and money to eat themselves witless across the way, as we were going to do in only a few hours.

Promptly at eight, we walked under the tall, stark, illuminated letters over the gate—F. POINT—and into a cluttered foyer. A cordial waiter led us into the dining room.

Like famous people, famous places are often smaller than you had imagined. This one was also more down at the heel. When her celebrated husband died, Mme. Point properly devoted her main energies to keeping his food standards high and the three stars shining, to the neglect of the decor. It seemed a shabby shrine—chairs upholstered in dark red plastic, faded cretonne curtains, a machine-embroidered tablecloth, silverplate worn partially black, thick cream-colored plates, and a menu bound in a red plastic that matched the chairs.

—For there was a menu, another change since her husband's day. He had served what he felt like serving, or what he felt his patrons should eat. Now there was a *prix-fixe table d'hôte,* seventy-five francs *sans vin,* and we ordered it, on the theory that it must be good or Madame wouldn't be pushing it. Besides, you never know what financial deep waters you may find yourself in once you start paddling in the direction of the *caviar extra* and the *écrevisses à la nage.*

BRIOCHE DE FOIE GRAS

DÉLICE PYRAMIDE

FILET DE TURBOT DE CHAMPAGNE

ou

SOLE FARCIE BRAISÉE AU VERMOUTH

CANETON NANTAIS GRILLÉ BÉARNAISE

ou

PINTADEAU POÊLE EN COCOTTE

GRATIN DAUPHINOIS

FROMAGES

GLACE ou SORBET     FRIANDISES     GÂTEAU MARJOLAINE

CORBEILLE DE FRUITS

It is to Madame's credit that on the tables there was no self-congratulatory literature attesting that the Prince of Wales had eaten there and found it marvelous. Or that Colette had, or Jean Cocteau, or Curnonsky. Or Joseph Wechsberg, who, as any food *aficionado* knows, immortalized M. Point back in 1953 in his *Blue Trout and Black Truffles*. (When a restaurant advertises itself at the point of impact, I think something within one dies, or at least gets a slight headache. Either you know these things before you go or you discover its excellences while you are there.)

The room was warm when we came in, and it grew quickly warmer by several caltos. (A calto is the number of sizzling-hot *tournedos* required to raise the temperature five degrees in a room containing seventy-seven perspiring diners, two of them in *aloha* shirts.) And the service was streamlined, in a homy sort of way—a tautly controlled confusion of white-coated lads shuttling like a lacemaker's bobbins under the sharp eye of the paunchy maître d', who chugged up and down the two strips of faded carpet between the three rows of tables, moving as though his feet hurt, and muttering to himself, but good-naturedly.

Our waiter was a friendly sort, too, and I was glad for that. He didn't have us feeling like a foreign body at the mercy of the rejection mechanism of the host, as some do, but enveloped us warmly. He heartily approved our selections. No matter that we had only to choose two out of two—how shrewd of me to choose the sole and the *pintadeau!* How perspicacious of Monsieur to elect the turbot and the *caneton!*

And so we proceeded from *chef d'oeuvre* to *chef d'oeuvre*, with frequent assists from a bottle of cold white Condrieu. The silky *foie*, the *délice* (mussels, cream, wine, spinach, pastry). The sole, entirely delectable, and the complicated turbot, busy as a wide-screen revival of *Ben-Hur*. The rich, moistly dark duck and the guinea hen. The *gratin dauphinois*, which is to the standard Lyonnaise potato as the rose petal to the cabbage leaf. ("Pace yourself," my husband muttered, his mouth full.)

And came the perfect winy Roquefort, and the creamy Reblochon. And the buttery honey-drenched *friandises,* a solid base for the massive digestive insult known as *gâteau marjolaine,* like licking the fudge pan twice. And, finally, the great bowlful of wild strawberries no bigger than peanuts, under the cumulous whipped cream . . .

It was a test, all right, a true final examination, two hours of dedicated, concentrated effort. It was quite a dinner. Indeed, *quite* a dinner. But we made it. And when we finished, we tidied ourselves with the heavy napkins the size of tablecloths, and stared at each other.

Finally, puffing a bit, we said our *au revoirs.* In the small front hall, Mme. Point bade us good night and we shook hands, that brisk no-nonsense one-chop of a French handshake. Then we made our way down the quiet street, weaving only somewhat, back to the hotel.

Never, I thought, had my taste buds been quite so cosseted and overwhelmed, or my digestive apparatus quite so perilously strained, I thought later on, taking an Alka-Seltzer just for luck. It had been, all in all, like having triplets—a basically fascinating experience, but you knew it would take time to get your figure back, and you wouldn't do it again in a hurry if you could help it.

Then, in the postoperative clarity the following morning, I thought back to it all, dish by dish. And that is when I realized that the sole—the sole braised in the vermouth—had been quite simply the best thing I had ever tasted, with the possible exception of my grandmother's lemon meringue pie when I was ten years old.

Phenomenal. What could I compare it to? Debussy? Or Shelley in his pure lyric vein? This is the sort of thing that can happen to you.

---

Now, back home, remembering both meals, trying to taste again those things in my mind, separately and in their entirety, I find that their message escapes me. Cooking is a lively art but a transitory one. And I think of George Lang, who wrote somewhere about his failure to decipher the hidden meaning of an eight-course Japanese banquet he had enjoyed. (It is a Japanese custom to incorporate a philosophic thought into a menu, on special occasions.)

It had been a superb meal he had had, but inscrutable, from its first course of figs in sesame paste with rice vinegar and crisped bonito crumbs, through baby corn fritters and sea urchins' eggs, all the way to the final golden-yellow watermelon and mixed pickles. Finally, the chef explained that the dinner had symbolized "the inevitability and fatefulness of experience, through nature's diversity and unity."

This had somehow eluded Mr. Lang, just as—I am afraid —some of the French nuances had eluded me. Great cooking, like great music, demands a great audience, and sometimes a great stomach.

Still, in this day of increasingly efficient group-feed, I believe it is moderately important that these things remain moderately important. Sometimes, now, in my own kitchen, as I start the frozen asparagus and the blender hollandaise, I remember with affection and awe that halcyon lunch, that memorable dinner.

And often, too, I think of Charles Narsès cooking away in his École de Cuisine, doggedly carving his swirling mushrooms and beating his egg whites before the docile class, so that one day another Charles Narsès can rise to take his place. A pilot light he is, helping to keep alive the general flame (but gently, turn it low, the sauce mustn't boil). And I view him and his confreres with respect, rather as I do the contemplatives of the church—off the busy thoroughfare, yet purposeful for all that, creating a pool of quite definite goodness for a naughty world to draw on.

# 13

---

## The Leeward Side of a
## Spouting Whale

*Which has the author moving from the sublime to
the possible, in a quite practical chapter*

With some people, a taste of the best is only disheartening.
Once he hears Menuhin, the tyro sorrowfully puts away his
fiddle; and when I tasted Mme. Point's *sole farcie braisée au
vermouth* in the preceding chapter, I knew I would never
cook fish again. Or, well, hardly never.

And so I seldom bring any exotic recipes back home,
which is probably just as well. Even the simplest foreign im-
ports can make trouble (like the French 7, which always
looks so traveled, I think, but I regretfully had to drop it
when the local postmistress told me it was no good for zip
codes). And in Brittany you add a little wine to your soup
dregs, which cheers up the soup dregs and tastes fine, but
here the waiter will look at you oddly.

Or take the matter of the black olives they grind to a
paste in Provence to serve with sweet butter and French
bread. After I'd used up the better part of an afternoon pit-
ting and grinding, it wasn't the same. Mine were Greek
olives, not Provence olives, and the bread was different, as
well as the scenery and the cast. I couldn't supply the old
Palace of the Popes across the way, or the gentle dusk of the
restaurant garden, or the waiter who looked like Jonathan
Winters. (*"Bon appétit, ce n'est pas moi qui paye,"* he
chortled happily, several times. A jolly fellow he was, and
candid, too.)

Accordingly, the few imported recipes in this practical chapter were comfortably acclimated here before I ran across them—always a good hedge against disaster—and the more generalized suggestions are mainly domesticated, too.

Quite often, these come along unexpectedly. For instance, I was making a speech one afternoon on the stage of a theater somewhere in Michigan. It was rather a big theater, and it is a small feeling to stand soul-alone in front of the wide Vista-Vision screen, which is covered by the curtain, and you wish it weren't—wish it were full of Omar Sharif and you were down there watching it, and it's a safe bet the audience does, too.

"You shut your mouth," a lady called, from way in the back, which didn't surprise me, though it was unsettling. Then I realized that she was only telling me how to chop onions without crying. She enlarged on the subject: you may not realize it, but your mouth is usually open at least a little bit—talking, singing, sighing, or breathing somewhat adenoidally. Be sure your mouth is tightly closed while you chop, she said, and you won't cry.

This was good to know, and I mentally filed it under 0 for tears, along with Chef Narsès's technique—he chopped so fast there wasn't time to cry—and someone else's (store your onions in the refrigerator, because cold onions are technically tearless), and my own (use freeze-dried or frozen chopped onions whenever possible).

Indeed, as someone must have pointed out before, travel is educational; and though the lessons may not look immediately valuable, you never can tell.

A friend of mine learned, around Fiji, that killer whales have a remarkably bad breath when they spout—even when they don't, probably, but it is when they're spouting that you really catch it, the way you do when someone heaves a windy sigh in a small elevator.

She discovered the fact when she was sailing, one day. Their boat came too close to this big fellow, who spouted at them. It was a killer, all right, and quite put them off their sandwiches. Thus, at the right time, this is a practical thing to know. Be sure you stay on the leeward side of a spouting whale.

And just one more item before this chapter becomes too gamy to keep, this one about skunks. I learned from a man in Montana that if your place is attractive to them, you can easily make it less so. Puncture a hen's egg with an icepick, inject a fleck of strychnine, then seal the hole with tape. Bury the egg where you've seen or smelled the skunk, and you won't see or smell him any more. I like to think that he detects it from afar and just keeps going, though I don't know what really happens.

I have noticed that travel teaches more about food than it does about housekeeping, unless you happen to be on a Fulbright, studying window-washing. This may be because housekeeping is generally what you do when you run out of other activities, not something you talk about. Also, good housekeeping, like good manners, is usually inconspicuous, as well as being one corner where Americans* have more to teach than to learn.

* For convenience in this book, I use American to mean a citizen of the United States, as most of us unfortunately do, to the considerable annoyance of twenty million Canadians, thirty-six million Mexicans, eighteen million Central Americans, and two hundred million South Americans. The trouble is that no satisfactory name for us has yet evolved, though there have been many suggestions, printable and otherwise. United Statesian is clumsy, Usanian sounds like the one hundred fourth element, and Usonan would be a pimple cream or a drug cure. Perhaps Tisotheenian is the best so far, from the first line of one of our national anthems.

In the big buildings in Mexico, I watched the janitors swab the tile with something that looked like a large limp canvas flag, swishing and swooping it aimlessly about. Though it didn't seem to make things look any worse, still, on the other hand . . . And I watched them wash their clothes in the irrigation ditches before spreading them carefully out to dry on the mud. And on a Taxco rooftop I inspected my hostess's clothes-drying invention, a fantasy of spikes, pulleys, and wires that could be variously arranged, she explained proudly, depending on whether she had a short maid or a tall one.

In a hotel near Loch Lomond, I was nearly blinded by the bright brass risers on the stairway. "How often do you polish them?" I inquired of the sturdy little factotum with the rosy-red knuckles. "Why, every day, mum," she said, in some surprise, and I was sorry I'd asked.

The best foreign housekeeping idea I've run across is, I think, the Thai spirit house. In Thailand, the spirit of the house is most important, as indeed it is anywhere, but there they take better care of it. Before a Thai moves home and hearth, he builds a birdcage-size house for the spirit to live in so that it won't feel dispossessed, else the family might not thrive happily together in the new one. Spirit houses might be a real help in our own country, it seems to me, considering our newly wandering ways.

Other than that, the best house ideas have come from comparatively nearby—three, for example, from a Philadelphia bachelor named Ben (bachelors are either superb housekeepers or terrible, no in-between):

1.   He automatically dropped his kitchen sponge into the dishwasher every time he washed dishes, and had as a result the perpetually freshest sponge I ever saw.

2.   He used his ice bucket to keep hot things hot—beans,

macaroni, rice, mashed potatoes. Filled it with hot water first.

3. He froze his Christmas-tree popcorn, using the same strings six years going on seven.

I borrowed the popcorn technique myself, rather to my regret. I've always thought that someday I would have a truly elegant Christmas tree—Swedish modern, or glass-and-bamboo, or something of the sort. But now, with several miles of frozen popcorn safely stored away, I see the smart tree go glimmering. Neva hoppen.

Possibly my best all-round household help came from the Great Smokies, near Gatlinburg, Tennessee, where the old log houses and cantilevered barns and sorghum mills and smokehouses still stand, mute witnesses of a simpler, harder day.

Posted under glass there is a letter of instruction that was found in one of the houses, written by a pioneer mother to her daughter sometime in the early 1800's. I find it helpful to reread when the sight of a vacuum cleaner seems more than mortal spirit can bear:

1. Build a fire in backyard to heat kettle of rain water.
2. Set tubs so smoke won't blow in eyes if wind present.
3. Shave whole cake lye soap in boiling water.
4. Sort things in three piles—white, colored, and rags and briches.
5. Stir flour in cold water to smooth for starch and thin down with boiling water.
6. Rub dirty spots on board, then boil. Rub colored things but don't boil. Take white things out of kettle with broom handle, then rinse, blue, and starch.
7. Spread tea towels on grass. Hang old rags on fence.
8. Pour rinse water in flower bed.
9. Scrub privy seat and floor with soapy water.

10. Turn tubs upside down. Put on clean dress. Comb hair. Brew up tea. Sit and rest a spell and count blessings.

But now to the recipes.

Choosing them wasn't easy, for I run into a great many. People often give them to me, and sometimes I wish I could dodge faster.

There was the matter of the Brandied Fruit Topping, from deep in East Texas. I was given a great apothecary jarful, with a sheet of involved instructions. This was on the sour-dough principle, except that you had to keep feeding it, accurately and punctually—cherries today, pineapple next week, sugar the next, and so on. Like motherhood, it was a career, not a one-shot, and I finally had to put it out for adoption.

I remember the British eleven-and-a-half-cent-per-day diet, too. In England, a friend pointed it out as an economical way to stay alive. Because the writing business involves more downs than ups, I've kept it, though I think it might better be called the Let's Go Jump off London Bridge Diet, or I'd Rather Be Dead Than Fed.

The diet was developed by a British research nutritionist, which is two strikes against it to start with. Predictably, the diet "meets all nutritional requirements," which is the real kiss of death, as anyone knows who ever ate a K ration.

At English prices at the time, the eleven-and-a-half-center consists of

| | |
|---|---|
| a scant lb. of self-rising flour | 8 cents |
| 2 ounces of lard | 2 cents |
| 1 four-inch carrot | 1 cent |
| 1½ large cabbage leaves | ½ cent |
| | 11½ cents |

Simmer everything together, then eat it all up, every day.

This is more expensive in the United States. I found that it went 16 cents, 8 cents, 6 cents and 1 cent over here, which totaled 31 cents, though my grocer kindly allowed that if things were that rough, he would throw in the cabbage leaves for free.

The first two recipes are from Williamsburg, Virginia, where I spent a raw, gray, wet couple of November days when sensible folk were at home by the fire.

Yet, this made for a more experiential sort of trip. It is easier, somehow, to feel part of a long-gone time and place when you slosh in from a sodden unpaved street to watch a bookbinder in knee breeches dye his end papers by a hot warming machine, without all the tourist tots trotting about in their tricorn hats.

At a tavern there I tried some quite authentic Sally Lunn. "Sally Lunn" came from *soleilune*—I imagine because they both rise and they're both yellow, which is about all you could say for the one I tasted. I was glad when a lady from Washington gave me her own recipe, which is quicker and better. You can tell by the name of it that it is simply a good recipe, not a difficult gourmet type, for the fancy recipes always put the name of the inventor last—Chicken Gravy Mrs. Jones, instead of Mrs. Jones's Chicken Gravy.

This one is called

## MARY MARGARET'S SALLY LUNN

     2   cups flour
     2⅓ tsp. baking powder
     1   tsp. salt
     ½   cup shortening
     ½   cup sugar
     3   eggs, beaten
     1   cup milk

Sift together the first three things so you won't have to do it when your hands are sticky. Then cream the shortening and sugar, and add the three eggs. Add the flour mix to this, a third at a time, alternating with the milk, a third at a time. Don't stir too much—it should be barely mixed and a bit lumpy. Pour it into an average-size loaf pan—oiled—and bake for half an hour at 425°. Then test it with a broom-straw, and maybe cook it another five minutes.

The second recipe is the Peanut Soup I had there, in Williamsburg, served from a handsome ironstone tureen that I'd rather have had than the recipe, though I am glad to have it, too. It's easy and good on a cold night.

## VIRGINIA PEANUT SOUP
### *4 to 6 servings*

| | |
|---|---|
| 2 cups chicken broth | 6 Tb peanut butter |
| 2 Tb chopped onion | 4 Tb ground or chopped pea- |
| 2 Tb butter | nuts |
| 2 Tb chopped celery | ¼ tsp celery salt |
| 2 Tb flour | ½ tsp salt |
| | 1 tsp lemon juice |

Sauté the chopped celery and onion in the butter till they're tender, add the flour and blend it, then add the chicken broth and simmer it for half an hour. Remove it from the fire, strain it, and add everything except the chopped peanuts. Heat it again to the boiling point, then serve it forth with the chopped peanuts on top.

Equally American is the next recipe, which I found in the quaint old Buckminster Fuller geodesic dome in Montreal when I saw Expo 67 in 71.

The Kiowa Indians are an artistic tribe who painted their daring exploits and other things on buffaloskins. They painted the celebration of the sun dance, and the coming of the white man, as well as the coming of the smallpox and the measles, which probably makes them the first pointillists, well ahead of Seurat; and it may be that their Fry Bread was handed down on a buffaloskin, too.

### KIOWA INDIAN FRY BREAD

3 cups flour
3 Tb baking powder
1¼ cup warm water
½ tsp salt

Knead the dough, roll it thin, then cut it in squares, strips, circles, whatever you like. Then deep-fat-fry them like doughnuts—370°—till they're brown on both sides. This makes the tepee smell good, as well as plenty of Fry Bread. I can't think precisely where it would fit into a menu, or, for that matter, where it wouldn't. It is good with soup, salad, chicken or ham. Or wherever you need ballast. Or just to eat.

The next two appetizers came from Ohio. One night, before I spoke in Cleveland, the hostesses had invited me to a dinner made from recipes out of my own two cookbooks.

This happens, sometimes, and with me it isn't a cause for major rejoicing. For one thing, I am familiar with those recipes; and for another, they generally taste better when someone else cooks them, so that I wonder what I've been doing wrong.

Fortunately, they changed their minds before any great harm was done. Among the canapés they served was Appetizer Pie, which tasted just as good later, when I made it myself. (This, by the way, is the criterion I have applied to these recipes—they still taste good unspiced by new faces and surroundings.)

## ROCKY RIVER APPETIZER PIE

1  8-ounce package cream cheese
2  Tb milk
1  2½-ounce jar dried beef, chopped fine
2  Tb instant minced onion
2  Tb green pepper, chopped fine
½  cup sour cream
¼  cup walnuts, chopped

Blend the cream cheese and milk. Add the onion, green pepper, dried beef, and sour cream. Spread it in a presentable pie pan, sprinkle with nuts, bake it for 15 minutes at 350°, and serve it hot with crackers.

The Taramasalata, next, came from Dayton. Winnie Stuart there said the only hard thing is to find the *tarama,* the pinky-orange roe imported from Greece by an occasional good specialty food shop or delicatessen. Also, she emphasized the importance of putting only half the mixture in the blender at one time; otherwise you'll have a real mess on your hands.

## TARAMASALATA

1  jar tarama (10 ounces)
10  slices of soft spongy commercial white bread,
slightly stale, crusts removed
1½  cups salad oil
3  lemons cut in chunks
½  onion, chopped

Dampen the bread briefly in water, then squeeze it out. Add everything else and blend it till smooth, in the blender. Serve it in a bowl with celery or chips or crackers to dip with.

———

It was in London that I first tasted Chess Tarts, but this version came from Chester Park, in Duluth. He said they were like the ideal girl—small, round, pretty, and rich—and I didn't argue, because I wanted the recipe.

## CHESTER PARK'S CHESS TARTS

*(makes 3 or 4 dozen, depending on the size you made them)*

- 1 cup butter
- 2 cups sugar
- 3 eggs, unbeaten
- 2 tsp vanilla
- 1 cup pecans or walnuts, chopped
- 1 cup raisins

Pastry enough for a two-crust pie, rolled out quite thin.

Cream the butter and sugar, add the eggs and vanilla, and beat it well. Add the nuts and raisins. Cut the pastry in rounds, about 3 inches in diameter. Tuck each one snugly into a small muffin tin, so it has a bit of a raised edge (or use a French tartelette pan). In each, put a heaping teaspoonful of the mixture, using slightly less than you think advisable. Otherwise it will run over and not look quite so pretty. Bake for 25 minutes at 375°. (If you run out of pastry before you run out of filling, freeze the rest of the filling for later.)

It was in Brittany, at an inn with the improbable name Ty Chupen Gwenn, that I met a charming French girl once-removed (she grew up in San Jose). Her name was Adalaine and she gave me a good simple apple recipe to serve with pork or chicken.

## CHERCHEZ LES POMMES

First, in a big iron frying pan, put an inch of water, a cup of white sugar, ⅓ cup of cider vinegar, 1 teaspoon of butter, and stir. Let it come slowly to a boil. Now peel and quarter four or five Gravensteins or Newton Pippins or, anyway, tart juicy apples. Reduce the heat so the liquid simmers, and put the apples in. Turn them with care occasionally. Cook till the liquid is absorbed and the apples look a bit glazed.

—As one does look after going a couple of rounds with the Lena Cocktail, the next recipe, and a smashing drink it is. The Lena was featured at the dinner meeting, in Denver, of the Women's Independent League of Do-Gooders, more handily known as the WILD party. They told me that when an Italian bartender created it in Japan at the recent bartenders' Olympics, it won him the title of World's Best Barman. Whether or not the Lena is the world's best drink, it seems to do everything a good drink is supposed to do. It was a small party but a good one, eight people, I believe, or possibly sixteen.

### LENA COCKTAIL
*(serves 4 once or 2 twice)*

Mix together

| | |
|---|---|
| bourbon | 5 oz. |
| sweet vermouth | 2 oz. |
| dry vermouth | 1 oz. |
| bitter Campari | 1 oz. |
| Galliano | 1 oz. |

Serve it over ice in an Old-fashioned glass, with a red cherry.

Then there is the pizza I tasted in Chicago—rather an odd pizza that doesn't know where its loyalties lie: Italy or Mexico. But I saw instantly that it is the answer for anyone who likes pizza better than making pizza crust. This is very quick and good, too.

## PERPLEXED PIZZA

1  6-ounce can tomato paste
⅔  can water
1  tsp oregano
1  tsp basil
1  tsp garlic salt
¼  cup chopped ripe olives
½  lb grated cheddar
½  lb grated mozzarella or Monterey Jack cheese
8  flour tortillas the size of salad plates or 4 big ones
odds and ends of sausage, mushrooms, et cetera—
    good but not essential

Mix the first six ingredients, then grate the cheese. Put the tortillas on a large baking sheet, or two large baking sheets. Spread with the sauce, then sprinkle on the cheese, then the et cetera, if you are using some. Bake at 500° for ten minutes. These are easier to eat if they're cut in pie-shaped segments after they've cooled a minute, and scissors are better than knives to cut with.

This brings us to the tenth recipe, as well as to scrummy tuck. Scrummy tuck is an Australian phrase meaning comfy grub, which is an English term meaning the homy, tacky things people enjoy eating occasionally but don't often admit to.

The Englishman who told me about this, as we drove around Kent in his Ford Ensign, kept his own version of it in the glove compartment. (English glove compartments don't contain gloves, either.) It was a comfortable, rather messy sackful of glucose jells (which I called gumdrops) and acid drops (which I called lemon drops) and Turkish delight, a milk-chocolate-covered orange jelly (which I called terrible). But he liked it by the handful, and his teeth seemed all right, all four of them.

A man I know likes to eat Eagle Brand Condensed Milk, out of the can with a spoon, though he doesn't talk about it much. Another wants plain milk straight out of the carton, and when his children catch him at it, they get cross. Kids are so germ conscious. But he says it doesn't taste as good from a glass. (You will note that scrummy tuck is often milky—soft creamy things, somewhat Oedipal edibles. Eating them out of the original container—you know what the psychologists would make of that—is frequently a part of the pleasure.)

Then another friend of mine periodically spreads a creamy cheese, like Brie or Philadelphia, on a Lorna Doone cookie. And eats it. I read, too, that the man who invented Noxzema enjoyed eating chopped peanuts and vanilla ice cream on his breakfast cereal. His grandson, on the other hand, enjoys eating Noxzema.

The reason I mention the matter is that Scottish oatcakes spread with an indecent amount of butter have been my own preferred scrummy tuck since I first tasted them in the Scottish Highlands, years ago. This is the exception that proves the rule: the recipe, which I got in Edinburgh, makes oatcakes that taste just as good as they did there—good, that is, if you like the taste of oatmeal and butter, not very good if you don't. I do, and so I try to keep some oatcakes handy for those unloved and unlovable times when one must comfort one's self.

## SCOTTISH OATCAKES

Mix together 3 cups of uncooked oats—instant or otherwise, it doesn't seem to matter—with a teaspoon of salt and ¾ teaspoon of baking soda. With your hands, work in 5 tablespoons of melted butter, not margarine, and a scant ¾ cup of hot water. This makes a firm paste that's easily rolled out on a lightly floured board till it's ¼ inch thick. Then cut it with a big round cookie cutter. Sauté them in butter* in a hot heavy skillet, about three minutes per side, or till they're golden. These bear up well in a closed tin can in the refrigerator. I've even taken some along for breakfast at hotels, or when I am a guest in someone else's house.

—Which brings up another point, as well as another recipe: the feeling of helplessness that can descend upon you in a strange kitchen (as well as in your own). When I find myself alone in someone else's, I usually can only stand there in bemused dismay, sure that I won't be able to find anything, and equally sure that I shouldn't try. Rather an invasion of privacy, it seems to me, like going through someone's dresser drawers.

As I am a house guest who gets up early, this reluctance to explore has lost me some mornings, unless the percolator is in plain sight and ready to perk. God bless the hostess who takes care of this the night before and also leaves a popcorn trail to the coffeepot.

Accordingly, when I stayed overnight recently at the home of my good friends Brandy and Ellie, in Milpitas, I was happy to find that he was up early, too, and cooking.

Brandy is a good-looking man, six feet three and 180 pounds, including his tennis elbow. He was born with a caul, which is allegedly a permanent protection against drowning. It must be so, for he hasn't drowned yet, though one time around the holiday punch bowl it was nip and tuck, and if his wife hadn't saved him, the caul probably wouldn't have.

---

* Clarified butter is best because plain butter burns so fast. Over low heat, melt a stick or two of butter till it's frothy, then strain it. The froth stays in the muslin or the old nylon stocking, and you use the other part.

However, he produced some interesting French toast of his own devising, so good that I want to include it here.

## BRANDY'S FRENCH TOAST

You start with a long slender loaf of French bread, the kind the French call a baguette, shaped like a somewhat flattened long salami. Cut it in 1½-inch chunks. Beat an egg with about ¾ cup of milk and a little salt. In this, marinate the chunks for an hour while you play tennis or go back to bed. Then come back and sauté the chunks in an electric skillet at 300°, using half vegetable oil of some kind and half butter or margarine. Serve with the usual syrup.

He also gave me a recipe that he'd come across in the Australian outback, an Australian Halloween dessert called "Boo-meringues." The taste, he said, returns to haunt you. This was going to be the twelfth recipe here, but I've misplaced it, and I looked everyhere, but not very hard.

# 14

---

# The Calories in the Caviar

Travelers find it easier to overeat than just plain eat, as a rule; and it isn't unusual to waddle back home with some undeclared pounds.

There are sound reasons for it. Those fleeting time zones bring meal hours around again with remarkable speed. Also, in dull places where they've rolled up everything else, you can still—as a rule—eat. Moreover, like children, travelers will often eat elsewhere what they wouldn't eat at home, and more of it. I may not pass this way again and what the hell, the traveler properly thinks as he reaches for another hot fresh bun when it's teatime in Devon, to slather with thick Devonshire cream and strawberry jam.

So it can add up to avoirdupois, abetted as it is by two other befuddling factors. For one, the traveler feels as though he is using up more energy than he is. Like the old lady who remarked, "If I sit real still, I don't feel a day over twenty," if the traveler sits real still, he'd hardly believe he's crossed all that country and become acquainted with so many cobblestones and customs men in only five short days. It is when he stands up that he feels like Rod Laver after the sixth set of singles, and translates the feeling into Skinny & Hungry. (But in general, sight-seeing uses up about as many calories as knitting.)

The other confusing thing is the miracle stretch fabrics. Stretch is precisely what they do, around their gently ballooning inmate, while inside them he feels the same as always.

It is troublesome enough to have to unload a fat suitcase, let alone six or seven fat pounds, which is easy to do, just let them alone till they've become part of the establishment. And so prevention is better than cure, though it isn't always easy.

I remember a bright morning aboard a Flying Dutchman flying from Oslo over fjords and snow and pine trees to Copenhagen. Breakfast was good black coffee—no cream, for that would have been fattening—with a haunch of poundcake worth its weight in butter, two brown-sugar-and-jam cookies, and a box of Dutch chocolates—just a small box, only a quarter of a pound—and I ate the whole thing.

Later on at lunch in Denmark, as we pondered the mysterious menu, our waiter assured us that "Delicious for Two" would be the perfect tidbit to tide us over till dinner. "Small but appetizing" is what we thought he said.

It turned out to be a great pewter platter of sausages, pork cutlets, duck, chicken, kidneys, glazed onion rings, glazed tomatoes, glazed crab apples, and a bale of dark salty potato chips, heaped like autumn leaves. I ate all that, too, and reflected, while adding some bitters to my schnapps because the waiter seemed to expect it, that this was a serendipitous dividend of not speaking the language. I wouldn't have missed it for the world.

So we undid a few buttons before going on to dinner—a slab of rare beef, as I remember, with good Danish beer and a hot, crusty, deep-fried Camembert cheese that was entirely rewarding.

There are worse things than being fat, and one of them is worrying about it all the time.

---

Before we get down to the gist of this chapter, it might be well to get some miscellaneous calorie items out of the way —take care of the canapés, so to speak, before the dinner.

Seven medium oysters are only 50 calories, while a cup of oyster stew is 225.

Chinese food is usually a good choice, though he who eats Chinese should skip egg roll.

A tablespoon of tartar sauce is 135 calories, probably more than the fish you eat it on.

A tablespoon of caviar is only 100 and, if you like caviar, well worth it. Have two.

Melon is fine, except watermelon. A small thin slice like a piece of bread has the thrust of a chocolate cream, while half a cantaloupe is a mere 50 calories.

Four stewed prunes with juice equal 200 calories; half a cup of strawberries equal 30.

Most French menus have an *entrecôte* that resembles an American minute steak. You can ask for it *sans sauce*.

An immersion heater (the small coiled affair that heats water fast for instant coffee in your hotel room) can also make bouillon to take the edge off hunger. You can carry changeable plugs for foreign outlets, and some bouillon cubes.

On hot days in beer countries, Vichy on the rocks with lemon peel is refreshing, too.

When in doubt, eat fish.

---

However, more important than these random facts are three fundamental suggestions:

1. Assuming you'll gain five pounds anyway, it is wise to take thirty days to lose five pounds before you go. Though you could lose them in ten days or so, they would likely bounce back like an echo; and the idea is to earn a good month's not thinking about it.

2. When traveling, eat something full of protein in the morning so you won't be too hungry at lunch.

This is a spin-off from the health-buff's dictum: *Make your biggest meal breakfast.* Eat a great energy-producing breakfast, they say, and a scanty lunch, then only clear broth for dinner, happy in the awareness that you've now used up all those calories so you can start tomorrow with a clear conscience and another huge breakfast.

It is sound advice, too, except that it disregards the fact that most sensible people would rather be shot. Either they can't stomach that much food in the morning, or they can stomach it nicely without impairing in the slightest their capacity for lunch and dinner.

And which good restaurants open at 7:00 A.M.?

Where does a bottle of wine fit in?

It was Adelle Davis who came up with a neat compromise solution. The thing to do, she says, is this:

> Sift together equal parts of dry food yeast and powdered milk. In little envelopes—one for each day of the trip—put ¼ cupful of the mixture. Pour it into your breakfast juice and drink it.

She admits the mixture doesn't taste exactly delicious. But then, neither do some juices. I've had orange juice in Paris that tasted like the Seine, and some in Africa that made the Seine look good. Also, various yeasts have different flavors. You can shop around in health-food stores before you go, to see which suits you best, though it is easier to hold your nose or just breathe through your mouth while you drink it.

Each packet is rich in protein-derived energy, you see, which keeps you from getting so hungry. You can lunch* informally on the run, then, sampling a specialty or two of the region, which otherwise you might never get to taste at all.

Indeed, it has long been a lament of mine that the specialty of the region is so seldom found on the menus of the region, especially in the United States. Not that it's hard to find clam chowder along the eastern seaboard, or abalone on the Monterey peninsula, or mahi-mahi in Hawaii, or corn in Kansas. But I'd like to see the figures, someday, on the percentage of frozen and canned versus fresh served by most of the local restaurants.

And I weep for the things that never make the menu at all. *Why can't we have some apricots for dessert, Mommie, like we saw on all those trees? Because they shipped them all to the cannery, Audrey; hush up and drink your frozen orange juice.* Or, for apricots, read walnuts in walnuttime, persimmons in persimmontime, papaws in papawtime, figs,

---

* Avoid the lunchtime sandwich if possible, in the U.S. because it is generally fattening and dull, and in Europe because it is either much bigger than you'd bargained for or so much smaller you eat six. Europe has never quite understood the theory and practice of the sandwich. Even the French don't know enough to put an *e* in sandwichs, or any butter or mustard, either. Just a loaf of bare French bread and a sliver of ham, except at the Pub in Paris, which specializes in English and American things. Their hamburgers look and smell like hamburgers, though I didn't try one, so I don't know. But I learned quite accidentally what they do to iced tea there. Though it looked and smelled like iced tea, when I was half done with it I felt an urge to put a lampshade on my head and sing comical songs, and so I asked the waiter, "Did you put gin in this?" *"Mais oui, madame,"* he said, in some surprise. As in "Doesn't *everyone?*"

black cherries. . . . In California, when the black cherries are big as Ping-pong balls, all wine-dark juicy-sweet flesh, the menus still feature ice cream, gelatin, and homemade pie from the Homemade Pie Mfg. Co. somewhere in New Jersey.

Europe is better, because their freezing and shipping facilities are worse, happily for anyone who wants to eat the beautiful white asparagus in Holland in asparagustime, or the wild strawberries in France, or the broad beans in broad-beantime in Rome. (And you might as well eat broad beans in broad-beantime, because everyone else does, including the round priests in their round black beavers and billowing black skirts, happily diving into their great heaping platefuls.)

It is mainly in the dessert department that parts of Europe fall down so badly on regional specialties, it seems to me. Portuguese bakeries, for instance, are a fat man's dream of heaven, replete with incredibly rich nut-laden pastries wholly unknown to the Portuguese restaurants and hotels, which automatically bring out an orange at desserttime, or the ubiquitous caramel custard known as "flan." ("I had a sort of custard last night," said the lady next to me at table, "so tonight I guess I'll try that flan.")

In Aix-en-Provence, home of the amiable almond-and-honey *calisson,* your chances of finding one in a restaurant are as good or as poor as your chances of finding a praline on Antoine's menu in New Orleans. Which seems a shame.

And so lunchtime is a good time to free-lance in the groceries, markets, and bakeries. It is a good time for street food, too—a hot roasted chestnut from a cart in New York, if it's winter, or a noodle from a Japanese noodle wagon, if you hurry—they are fewer now—or a *tapa* or two with a glass of wine in Barcelona.

One of the best lunches I've had was a Mexican street-wagon clam cocktail, which so impressed me that I made a note of how the little boy prepared it.

### AJIJIC CLAM COCKTAIL

First get yourself a two-wheeled white pushcart. Then chop clams, push a heap into a paper cup. Squeeze an entire lime into it, add the clam juice, a shot of garlic salt, catsup, and six generous shakes of Tabasco. Stir, grinning widely, and serve it forth.

Finally, then, to

3. Don't get fat on things that are only so-so; at least get fat on the things you like a lot.

For instance, the ordinary pallid cream soup is hardly worth the 200 calories per cup. But some soups are. In a Northern European mountain inn, should you stumble in out of the snow on a cold white winter's day, toward the blazing hearth in a low-ceilinged wood-paneled room twinkling with calico and copper and candlelight—what the Danes call *hyggelig* and the Germans call *gemütlich*—where the Gosser Bräu flows like the Danube only cleaner, and they bring in a steaming tureen of sour-cream-potato-and-mushroom chowder, it will be more than 200 calories per cup and well worth it. Prudence must at all times be tempered with common sense.

Also, it is entirely possible, remarkable as it may seem, to lose weight on things you like a lot. Somewhere I read some impressive testimony to this effect, by a girl who lost five pounds on a cruise.

She drank Chablis instead of a cocktail before dinner because she liked Chablis better anyway. Then she ate mainly fresh shrimp and lobster, green turtle consommé, caviar, *filet mignon,* asparagus, cheese, strawberries, raspberries, fresh pineapple, and melon. She also swam early every morning in the ship's pool. Besides getting exercise, she found she had more men to herself that way, for not many women swim before breakfast. This may have provided an additional bulwark against the eventual temptation of the strudel and the waffles.

To sum up, then, a sound approach to the weight problem is this: provide yourself with a five-pound margin before takeoff, then dutifully eat the early-morning protein supplement, which lessens the likelihood of eating an outsize lunch, while guaranteeing the energy needed later for a good sprint to the caviar bowl.

*Still ran Dingo—Yellow Dog Dingo—always hungry, grinning like a rat-trap, never getting nearer, never getting farther.* —Just So Stories

PART FOUR

# Some Other Places

# 15

## Let's Hear It for the Package Tour!

"I was just lucky," said the plump lady in the turquoise polyester pants suit. She was also wearing some very lively earrings, ivory dice on short gold chains, and her name was Mrs. Moone. "I never had a kid that was a swallower."

She looked accusingly down and around the big long table in the big long dining room of the boat that was taking us all from Spain to Morocco. "Some kids are, you know. Swallow anything. Sani-Flush, Purex, you name it, they'll swallow it. Either they swallow or they don't swallow, and that's *it*."

The two women across from her nodded agreement.

"But I never had a swallower," Mrs. Moone said. "Thank God."

She was sixty-five, she said, three times a widow, two sods and a grass, with three children, nine grandchildren, and a blonde tint that kept turning red on her, she explained, if she didn't watch it.

We were getting acquainted over lunch, all of us members of the Morocco Tour Group that had gathered that morning in Málaga, bound for a six-day tour of the Imperial Cities.

We had never been on a tour before, my husband and I; and in this day of the affinity group and the charter flight, that is about like admitting you've never been vaccinated.

This wasn't one of the new Now tours. Not the Saddle-Up Tour around Italy, or the Ecology Tour of the Upper Nile, or the Psychic Tour of Great Britain, featuring a daily séance plus an afternoon at Stonehenge with the Chief of Britain's Most Ancient Order of Druids. Nor was it the Hot Pants Tour of Japan, where couples split up midway and take off for all sorts of genial doings, or the Nudist Tour (Yugoslavia) where they just take off.

It wasn't even one of those wholesome constructive tours, like summer school, bright with brass rubbings and university lecturers and archaelogical digs. (Whatever you dig these days, you seldom dig it alone.)

This was only a plain, old-fashioned, everything-included package tour, bags in the hall by 7:15 A.M., the whole group moving together from sight to sight to bus to bed, moving in a body, like maggots, as a friend of mine always adds, and I haven't been able to get her to stop it.

Our reasons for being there were fairly simple: I wanted to find out what is so bad about the package tour. As the most casual travel-book reader knows, package tours are held in low regard, yet they seem to continue in good supply; and this puzzled me, the way the gumdrop situation always has. That is, are green gumdrops in the majority because everybody likes them, or because nobody does?

At any rate, few people admit to having taken a package tour, or if they do, they are shamefaced about it, the way women used to say "Of course, I'm only a housewife. . . ." Or else they say it was the first package tour they ever took and they went out of curiosity, the way I just did.

So here we all were, about to go see the four North Moroccan cities that have been the seat of the government there, at one time or another. They passed it around like a hot rock, actually, Fez to Marrakech to Meknes to Rabat, and when a capital moves around that much, it's apt to leave a great many tombs and so forth behind, as we were shortly to find out.

The dining room bounced gently on the deep-blue-green Mediterranean as the help bustled about, and I noticed that the passenger next to me was wearing the hunted look of a man in a foreign situation in which something is expected of him but he doesn't know what the hell what. Then I saw his problem. He had eaten well and truly of the first course—the salami, ham, deviled eggs, rolls, and tomatoes—and now the rest of the meal was arriving.

"I told you that was only for openers," his wife said cheerfully, as the waitress brought in twenty-three platefuls of chicken with rice and green peas. It was just as well he didn't know about the delicious canned figs and stale Nabiscos that were still to come.

Their name was Hamilton, Binnie and Charles, Grand Rapids, real estate. First vacation in years, but now the kids were off and running, Charles and Binnie were at long last going to see a few places. She had lively blue eyes and short, curly brown-gray hair. He was tall, with a tall forehead and a pleasant expression.

Next to them was a short, sallow French-Canadian couple, no English between them. And a big-boned newly divorced secretary from Chicago, Ione Jones, who wore great round glasses the size of salad plates and a new leather coat, probably Barcelona. (People's itineraries can often be deduced from bits and pieces that stick to them.) And there was a retired dean of women, a Mrs. Hutteman, who asked terribly sound questions and wore a brownish chignon that nearly matched her hair. And a fat red-faced Argentine couple, and a hearty nurse on holiday, Sally Something, who was allergic to eggs—though of course we didn't know all these things immediately. Any tour group is as anonymous as any elevator load, till the second or third day out.

There was also a hardware man from Madison, Wisconsin —Al Horner, a dour, silent type—with his wife, Ellen, a thin, anxious little thing in a bright red pants suit that didn't do quite what she must have had in mind. She whispered a lot. ("I do think travel is so stimulating," she whispered behind her hand, during the boat lunch, and I murmured right back that it certainly was.)

Then there were some other people that I never quite sorted out, and there was also Mrs. Henry Teddisch, of San Diego. She was a militant lady with one of those larger-than-life-size faces and solid convictions. You couldn't miss Mrs. Teddisch, though most of us eventually wished that we had.

"I'll have milk, if it's pasteurized," she said now, as the waitress set two tall carafes of white wine on the table. "One must maintain one's calcium intake," she said, smiling to show her good strong teeth.

"I never had any calcium in my teeth anyway," Mrs. Moone said. "It all went to my knees." She laughed and threw her head back so the jiggling earrings jiggled some more, then reached for the wine and poured herself a generous knock.

At any rate, there were twenty-three of us, including our handsome young Spanish guide, Luis, on leave from the University of Madrid, and broad-backed Antonio, the bus driver, each of us duly sworn and committed to getting our bags out in the hall each morning at 7:15, most of us taking an inscrutable snapshot of the Rock of Gibralter as we slid past it in the fog, after lunch.

It was late in the day when we docked at Tangier, that venerable crossroads where the Mediterranean meets the Atlantic and Europe meets Africa and boy meets girl in the kasbah, both wearing blue jeans and granny glasses. Bright, sun-baked, and flat-topped, the town was bustling as we drove in the bus we'd brought with us to the Station de Fumigation des Vegetaux. People flocked around as we pulled up—white turbans and dirt-brown djellabahs and red fezes and Ali Baba bloomers and madras bedspreads, Moslem Africa, Christian Europe, hippie America.

I think it is always a great moment when you see your first *National Geographic* page come to life in living color. Ellen Horner thought so, too. She whispered behind her hand, "Isn't it just like the Bible? Honestly, it's just like the Bible," and it was, too, if you edited out the bus and the Coke signs and the buildings and gas pumps and so on. The tourist must learn, we found, to keep his eye on the doughnut instead of the ever-widening hole.

Tangier was only a springboard for the Imperial Cities that lay ahead, and so no one did any real exploring. After the first of the formidable five-course dinners included in the package, we went to bed at a reasonable hour, uneasily aware of 7:15 the following morning. (For the record, not one of us missed getting the bags out in the hall on time. I never saw what happened to them after that, but I think our big bus driver came around on tippy-toes, like the tooth fairy, to spirit them back into the bus.)

The next morning we gathered for breakfast in the dining room of the big hotel (which was, by the way, fairly typical of our lodgings for the rest of the week—modest rooms and a lavish lobby and coffee that was barely too thin to plow).

"They say Moroccan leather isn't much good any more," said Mrs. Moone, reaching for the butter. She had changed her dice earrings for some that looked like wind chimes, but they still jiggled. "You're supposed to spit on your finger and rub it," she said, "and if the color comes off, don't buy it. That's what they say."

"Yes, and the only really good buys are in the native

places where nobody knows how to mail anything," Ione said. "Or *won't* mail anything. Like Mexico."

(It became apparent, early, that "they" are important though invisible members of the package tour. They say, Don't miss so-and-so. They say, Skip such-and-such. This is the jungle news that comes via the long strong grapevine all over the world, a couple of million tendrils feeding the Tourist Word into the main stem. This is one of the many advantages of the package tour, too, for otherwise, I don't know how you would learn all these things.)

The rest of us nodded wisely, as though it were old stuff.

"It's like anything else," Mrs. Moone said, largely. She said it quite often, I noticed, one of those fat, loose remarks that seem to settle down over everything, like a collapsing tent.

Thoughtfully, we chewed our *croissants* and watched a neighboring tableful of tourists wearing MICHIGAN buttons make their own coffee out of the hotel's hot water and a jar of U.S. instant they had among them. Then we finished our own muddy brew and hit the road.

It was a middle-size bus we were traveling in, nothing fancy but built for hard wear, like our bus driver. And almost immediately, Mrs. Teddisch from San Diego made her presence felt. It developed that while the rest of us were finishing breakfast, she had pre-empted the entire spacious front seat, which was clearly marked on the guide's chart as belonging to the Horners. We all considered this unfair of Mrs. Teddisch, or, as Ione put it, cruddy. But Luis apparently sensed that he couldn't throw her out. Not only was she big, she was also the kind of woman who gets what she wants, and what she wanted was the leg room afforded by the front seat, where she could see best and hear most and be first out and first back in to sit down again. (When she was also first on our bus to get the galloping bleeps, later, in the gamiest part of the Marrakech medina, we were all quite pleased.)

And so Ellen Horner ended up across the aisle from me, whispering and crocheting. She favored pastel wool jerkins in a large-hole pattern that worked up fast, she said, and she liked to chat while she worked.

We moved on down the two-lane tarmac, toward the Atlas Mountains and Marrakech.

Morocco, as I noted specifically in my notebook, is where they wave bye-bye. On the coast, where the French resorts are, with names like Tahiti and L'Auberge and Les Paumes, they play soccer. But inland, the big outdoor sport is waving bye-bye, little kids and grownups alike, all with glorious all-out grins, waving hard as the bus goes past, sometimes even waving with both hands.

It was hard-scrabble country, starting out, and lonesome, too. Only an occasional solitary Arab shared the road, plodding along beside his small donkey or riding it sidesaddle because of his billowing skirts.

"This is an entirely agricultural area, is it not?" Mrs. Hutteman asked, pencil poised over her notebook. Luis listened to the question, thought carefully, and allowed that it was.

"Where are these *fellaheen* going?" she asked. It was clear that she'd done her homework.

Luis explained that they were either bound for a fair or commuting to work. He said the *fellahin*'s land was often in several ribbons, miles apart, because Moslem inheritance laws say that land must be divided equally among heirs. With all that dividing down through the generations, the strips shrink ever narrower. A *fellahin* can end up with some far-flung bits and pieces, and nothing but donkey or shanks' mare to travel on. Certainly we didn't see any fat *fellaheen*.

And I thought, as Luis explained all this, that here was another advantage of the package tour—other people being
there to ask sound questions you might not think of yourself.

It is always a taut moment in a foreign country waiting to
see if your English-speaking guide speaks English—as of
course Luis did, though he didn't hear English too well, and
we found, early on, that it was best to let him carry the ball.

His specialty was history, and there is a great deal of it
going around over there—riots, airport strafings, and at-
tempted assassinations, although this wasn't the history Luis
expounded. The package tour, I noted, seems mainly concerned with what was, not what is, and it is certainly more
restful that way. Probably in the year 2200 they'll have
worked up to 1971.

However, our Mrs. Hutteman knew a great deal of past
history, too—could even distinguish Moulay Idriss from
Moulay Ismail and all the rest of the Moulays, which is like
knowing John Adams from John Quincy from James Trus-
low, et cetera. She and Luis seemed to understand each other
nicely.

And so he erupted, spasmodically, into molten chunks of
Spanish, then Spanish-English, then Spanish-French. (Once,
Binnie Hamilton muttered behind us, "Did you ever notice
how dumb people look on tour buses? That's because half
the time they're listening to some language they don't understand.") Then he slumped forward and napped awhile,
knocked out by his own prose, or perhaps by his extracur-
ricular activities the night before, for Luis and Ione from
Chicago had seemed friendly right from the start.

With the local guides, it developed later, our language
hurdles were higher. In Casablanca, it was a Mustafa Hamud
whose bobbing fez and billowing skirts we dogged as we
tried to make out what he said. At first it was confusing, how
the Arab tongue turns our long *e* into a short *i*, though we

cracked the code after Mustafa had pointed out a number of old sidder sillings. And vice versa: our short *i* becomes a long *e,* we learned, as Mustafa tut-tutted over the women who had deserted their caftans for short skirts. Their meanies, he said, barely covered their sits, and true enough.

And so we drove steadily south, then inland, past cactus and cork trees, heading toward the foothills, where clumps of fuzz dotted the dim green, like old wool that had pilled, till gradually the colors warmed—crimson poppies and geraniums, and hot gold buttercups under a postcard sky, with white storks standing on the adobe huts that had only holes for windows because of the hot desert wind.

Four cities in six days is no small challenge, or so we found it; and what remains to me is a bright montage.

There was Rabat, the bright white city where the government lives at the moment, full of petits taxis—so tiny they only maim you, someone explained—and the red-pantalooned palace guards, looking quite as solemnly comical as they do outside Buckingham. And Fez, the old, gray city. And rose-red Marrakech, Marrakech of the jacaranda and the date palms, the Djemaa el Fna, and the pigeon pie.

And Meknes. What color was Meknes? I remember that Meknes is where somebody's shower backfired into the room next door, which happened to be ours. I remember that distinctly.

We saw a good many mosques. This tour stressed things like that, as I suppose most tours do. Though at home you don't customarily plunge around from church to cathedral and back again, unless you're the parish priest, tours seem to assume that that's what you want to do when you go traveling. I thought that a parent-teacher's meeting or an old folks' home or a whorehouse or a caftan factory might be interesting, too.

But it could have been worse. It was Charles Hamilton who observed that it was a real plus factor that Moslems only point out their mosques and won't let you into them. (He had brought along his soft spongy-soled museum boots but never once had to put them on.) We were permitted to enter only one, already defiled by unbelievers, I think, so that it didn't matter any more.

It was most interesting, too, with never a pew or an ikon or a hymnbook to tell you that you were in church. The only clue was a collection box. Even that was hard to spot, actually, in all the splendor—the tile, the alabaster, the jeweled mosaics, the ivory filigree, the fretwork, the plaster lace, all in an overwhelming geometric dazzle, bathed in a golden light like sun through honey, a celestial custard.

And we saw mausoleums. And gardens.

I remember especially the quiet rose-tree garden at the Saadian Tombs. My husband was taking pictures, and seeing Ellen sitting on a bench with her crochetwork, I sat down beside her, trying to think the thoughts you think you ought to think at the tomb of someone who had it made once but doesn't have it made any more, or else has it thoroughly made now, all depending on how you look at it.

Just then Mrs. Hutteman stopped to point out that the rose trees were looking seedy. If they asked her, she said, they should wrap the trunks in burlap. That's what she did some summers, even in Minneapolis, where it wasn't half as hot, either. We had quite a discussion about it, touching on rhododendrons, too, and dahlias, which I have never had any luck growing at home. It is another advantage of the package tour that there is always someone to talk to.

And we saw great walls and old palaces. In one palace we learned that the old kings didn't sleep on king-size beds, the way you'd expect, but only on ordinary double beds and hard ones, at that. Some of us tried them to see. Still, the old king had two of them, our guide pointed out, one for the lady of the nighttime, one for the lady of the daytime.

"So what's changed?" Ione muttered. She seemed rather disillusioned. I hoped she and Luis were getting along all right. (I had noticed that whenever he was nearby, she didn't wear her glasses.)

But Mrs. Teddisch had her own opinions about the affair. At one rest stop, lined up at the w.c., we were surmising, as ladies will—Binnie, Mrs. Moone, and some of the rest of us. Mrs. Teddisch looked around to make sure Ione wasn't there. "That girl has a sex problem," she said darkly. "You can always tell."

"Oh, I don't think so," I said, and Binnie didn't think so, either.

"My grandmother had a sex problem, too," Mrs. Moone contributed. "My grandfather kept trying to get into bed with her," and she laughed and laughed, and so did Sally Somebody, the hearty nurse whose name I never did quite catch.

Then I remember our first camel stop—a camel stop is when you stop to look at a camel—at a corner lot outside Rabat. Mrs. Hutteman explained to the group, in her clear voice, that camels don't carry water in their humps, they carry it in their bloodstreams, just like anybody else. This seemed a shame, for it rather took the poetry out of the camel, and this one had very little to begin with—a verminous-looking fellow he was, with a breath that would wither a date palm. For one dirham you could travel six paces on his back, led by a gentleman in a red fez, though only the fat Argentine couple took advantage of the opportunity. They took movies of each other every chance they got, and we could tell there were going to be some high old times next winter in Buenos Aires.

Dozing Arabs leapt to attention the second our bus sagged to a stop, any stop—rest stop, coffee stop, camel stop, or just plain stop. There they were, surging about, their merchandise at the ready.

Mrs. Moone bought one of nearly everything, and what she'd miss, Binnie Hamilton didn't. Plastic scimitars, plastic donkeys, crocheted woolly fezes, sacks of oranges, chocolate bars, leather bracelets, copper bracelets . . .

Binnie returned to the bus once with a clutch of barbecue skewers. This is Morocco's chief national product and never mind what you read about farming, it's barbecue skewers, tied in clumps of a dozen, and weighing about five pounds apiece in the bottom of a suitcase.

"How much?" asked her husband, his lip curling faintly.

"I don't know," Binnie said, and her voice was crisp. "I held out my money and they took some."

But all the female passengers assured her that they were splendid barbecue skewers. (It is still another advantage of the tour that other women are on it. Feminine reassurance about a purchase often helps; and few of us are so foolhardy as to level with a "Well, you can always give them to somebody," because we never know when we'll be needing similar support, ourselves.)

It was later on in the shrill Marrakech medina—the native market—that Mrs. Moone and Binnie stopped buying one of everything, there being more everything than they had, presumably, counted on.

The place was a torrent of brown faces, black veils, white veils, white turbans, dingy robes, and kids, kids, kids, streaking like minnows, racing about, dodging the tourists and the little burdened burros, who slipped and stumbled over the cobbles while the shouting porters prodded them with sticks.

We raced, too, up, down and around, though ancient

alleys like dank old urinals, past Le Bain et Douche Cali-
ente, past man-made caves lit only by white turbans and
shiny eyes, following our shepherd in the bright red fez,
tourist flocks hard upon the next flock's heels, figures in an
incipient mob scene or a free-for-all barn dance. In we come
and out they go, swing your camera with a do-si-do—and
don't lose Mustafa, who will lead you circuitously but without fail to the bazaar where he gets the best rebate, to an
Aladdin's basement full of silks, silver, copper, slippers,
caftans, trays, ribbons, hats, nuts, rugs, hides, bracelets, pins,
lamps, pistols, muskets, pills, potions, perfume, spices, obscure leather items, wild hardware, anything and everything
to buy, sell, swap, steal. . . . This is where Binnie and Mrs.
Moone threw in the towel and only stared.

It was in Marrakech, too, that we saw the Square of the
Dead, the Fun Place in Fun City, where everybody comes—
mountain Berbers (big strapping males swinging along holding hands, which seems to be the Arab way) and desert
Bedouins and tourists from everywhere—to see the splendid
goings-on, the tumblers tumbling, the fire eaters eating fire,
the snake charmers charming snakes. And they were doing
all these things, but it didn't seem to be one of their better
days. The tumblers achieved a certain accidental effect, as
though they'd been tripped, but they were quick to pass the
tambourine. And one lad drank boiling water—boiled it on
his sterno stove and drank it down like a milkshake—while
another shoved long metal rods up his nose. ("Disgusting!"
Mrs. Teddisch said, in ringing tones, though he clearly
thought it was sensational.)

The snake charmers were a little disappointing. Still, it is
probably hard to make much of an act out of a couple of
zonked cobras and a dishpan, because snakes don't do anything conclusive; and if they did, the act would be over. And

so the owner just gives them a mild poke, and the snakes stick their tongues out, and the owner sticks *his* out and passes the collection plate. . . .

It was a pleasure for all of us, I think, to get back to the hotel late in the day and talk it all over, at dinner.

Right here, by the way, is another undoubted advantage of the tour group: its humanizing effects on husbands and wives who are temporarily out of conversation except for "Don't tell me you lost the room key again."

A big feature of the travel landscape, if you've ever noticed, is the lumplike couples, the husband becoming lumplike sooner than the wife does; but the condition is infectious, and before long she's bound to catch it, too. Though actually these couples are everywhere, they are particularly noticeable in festive restaurants, the wife making valiant efforts to sparkle (embarrassed, if the truth be known, that they look so indubitably married) while he sits and chews to the haunting rhythm of the gypsy fiddles, by the light of the flaming *crêpes*. But it is hard to sparkle alone for very long, and so she finally subsides, to sit and chew, too. As my daughter remarked sadly when it rained on her sixth-birthday picnic, "It seems like a terrible waste of balloons." But on a package tour, people generally act livelier than they feel, which can be a help.

And something else—people probably see more sights than they'd have seen on their own. Take this same couple: they probably aren't pretending any more, at least about minor things like sight-seeing. He knows she's not going to cry if she doesn't get to visit the new dam—knows, in fact, that it ranks about seventy-fifth on her list of priorities. And she knows he won't have to be chained to the bedpost to keep him out of the native embroidery exhibit; that he'd

probably pay good money to avoid it. And so, if left to themselves, the two might have a comfortable drink on the hotel
verandah.

But on a tour this isn't sporting or even sensible, especially on a package tour that's all paid for. They feel duty-
bound to shape up and get cracking. Accordingly, they both
see the dam and the native embroidery, plus numerous other
things. Indeed, an appealing feature of the package tour is
the way it fits the puritan ethic, some of it being rather a
pain, which is good for you, like rhubarb and soda in the
springtime.

And so all of us were lively, and there were no real marital crises in our group—only one close call when Binnie
Hamilton got lost in a market (or so Charles assumed) and
missed the bus back to the hotel. As it turned out, she knew
perfectly well where she was and what she was doing—just
spending some more money—and murmured that he'd be all
right as soon as she apologized to him for his stupidity,
which he was.

Indeed, we were a congenial group, especially at meal-
times, as we shoveled our way through the couscous. Among
us, we scraped together enough French to include the
French-Canadian couple. It seemed he was in the artificial
insemination end of the cattle business, which was interesting, though hard to inquire about in French. And Ellen
Horner's husband wasn't as sour as he seemed—was quite a
conversationalist, really, if you stuck to hardware. He said
half the time he didn't know if he was running a hardware
store back home or a gourmet gift shop. My God, he said,
the turnover in fondue pots alone would make your eyes
pop. You had to stay on your toes, he said.

And then, after dinner, we'd usually stroll in the hotel
garden, if it had one, or down a broad eucalyptus-bordered

avenue in the soft dark, the shops all shuttered and secre-
tive, the feel of the mountains and the desert closer at nighttime than in the broad day.

And then there was belly-dance night.

I've been saving belly-dance night for the last, because
you shouldn't release the pigeons and run up the flag till the
end of the act. But now I'm here, I have an uneasy feeling
that there weren't any pigeons in the crate to begin with, and
my flag seems to be stuck.

The truth is, the Moslems don't really care for belly
dances. Left to themselves, they don't go out very often,
except to a café for some mint tea, and it wouldn't occur to
most of them to go watch somebody shimmy in public. They
prefer that a girl save her shimmying for home.

But it occurred to some travel agent or to Morocco's own
chamber of commerce that tourists might be happier if they
could go watch a belly dancer dance. And so, never averse
to turning an honest dirham, the Moroccans set awkwardly
about it and hired some halls.

Our belly-dance hall that night was brightly lit, like a
church basement readied for the chicken-potpie supper. Our
small tables faced the stage, where a lute and a fiddle and a
flute and a facile drummer played a good long overture.

At last a large Berber woman in dusty black came on and
sang, her mouth opened wide to show some magnificent gold
teeth. She was followed, eventually, by the *pièce de résist-
ance,* a honey-skinned belly dancer in a spangled bikini. She
belly-danced, and in the best tourist-trap tradition brought
the audience into the act—our fat Argentine, anyway, who
stuffed napkins into his shirt at strategic points and did some
bumps and grinds while his wife took more movies.

"Thasha trouble, not enough people getting kicked out of
enough places," Ellen Horner said loudly. She had been

adding Scotch to her mint tea, probably on the reasonable supposition that anything would improve it.

"Shut up, Ellen," her husband suggested.

"It's like anything else," Mrs. Moone said, with an expansive wave of the hand. . . .

And so, the next morning, the sun rose rosily over Marrakech as we made our way back up north, to venerable Meknes and Fez, and saw Volubilis, too, the old Roman city where fifteen thousand people lived once and now no one lives at all, where we walked about in the high windy quiet, and even Mrs. Hutteman had no questions to ask.

By the end of the fifth day, we all showed signs of wear—a spot here, a run there, a button missing, the hair lank and even the wig abandoned, the sideburns fuzzier (when a man has to get his bags out in the hall by 7:15, there is little time to play with the sideburns).

And when we'd once more found Málaga, approximately where we'd left it, I reflected that they should hand out service ribbons—something, anyway, to mark us as Package Tour Veterans of Four Imperial Cities (even though we couldn't quite remember which was which), all in six days, not to mention a mosque, a belly dance, two currency changes, three religions, four medinas, five *medersas,* seven tombs, eight *souks,* fourteen ponderous *prixe-fixe* meals, and all that couscous.

All in all, I reflected later, the package tour has its pluses and its minuses. It is a good way to see places you don't particularly care to, and there is a lovely restfulness about letting George do all the scutwork. No decisions, no responsibilities—how many other segments of your life can you say that about? Anything that takes care of all that baggage while it insulates you from all that culture shock can't be all bad.

And yet, when someone asks me if we've seen Morocco, I don't know quite what to say, except, Well, in a way . . . for I'm mainly aware of the cobbles we left unturned. Like a chastity belt, the package tour keeps you out of mischief but a bit restive for wondering what you missed.

Someday perhaps I'd like to see Morocco. Someday, too, we want to drop in on Ellen Horner's brother-in-law in Sacramento. He does wood carving and his wife knows a great deal about tropical fish, and they really sound awfully nice.

# 16

## To Keep the Mind Smiling

A Japanese tiger cat is helping me as I work, this early morning—a Hawaiian cat, rather, of Japanese ancestry. His name is Kolohe, which is Hawaiian for nuisance, and he goes with the house where we are house-sitting for a few weeks on the island of Maui—goes in and out of it at a great rate, for he seems to have a great many responsibilities.

Kolohe was a half-dead kitten when his present family found him under a hedge with his throat cut, two springs ago. Now he is a fine figure of a cat, an angular, silk-muscled, conversational cat who seems to take a continuing sunny pleasure in his reprieve. He divides his time efficiently between the Buddhist temple next door and the study here in this borrowed house, perhaps feeling a real obligation to make something of himself after such a close call.

Now he pads delicately through the shuffle of papers on the desktop, stopping from time to time to touch one with a tentative paw and meditate for a moment, much as I have been doing. Then he turns his attention to the typewriter as I type. He attacks the ribbon, bats the type bars into a stiff corsage, and—finally—subsides into my lap to knead my nightgown, the claws just bearably retracted into the pink cushions of his neat white feet.

"Go climb a palm tree," I suggest.

"Niao," Kolohe says, which is how I can tell he is Japanese. That and his eyes, which lack the second fold of the Caucasian eye, and are more elliptical than round.

But presently he reconsiders—sleeks down to the lauhala mat (this is an easy little shoes-off Hawaiian-style house) and leaves by the front door, where the wind bells tinkle a bit in the early breeze, then vanishes around the papaya tree. Probably going out to shadowbox a low-hanging hibiscus somewhere—he enjoys that—or over to help the neighboring priest with the early-morning service.

It is cool and warm and velvety out there at seven o'clock, the sun still behind the dark mountains. But a bit later, higher, it slants down the rounded shoulder of the big Buddha in the yard and paints a brighter green path across the grass to the temple door.

Kolohe usually sits a respectful distance between the two. He sits there quietly, just an ear flickering, as cats will do when they hear something inexplicable but interesting.

I thought this would be a good place to write about Japan —in this house, on this Hawaiian island. It has the right sort of feeling and is, in a way, reminiscent. There are so many Japanese in the rich racial mix here, and so much of surface Japan around—incense and chopsticks (only I learned they call them *hashi*) and kimonos among the muumuus, and in the supermarkets as much prepackaged Japanese *shirataki* as Kraft macaroni and cheese and Hawaiian poi.

And the Japanese keep coming. The tourists pour off the planes like peas shucked out of a pod by some big thumb, then into the buses and on to the hotels, if they don't go stay with Cousin Kiyoshi, who started a small camera store here twenty years ago and is doing nicely.

Japanese honeymoon couples are everywhere, too, taking pictures. Yesterday as we picnicked, the palm-studded park was thick with new brides and bridegrooms posing and snapping each other simultaneously from under their respective trees, then hurrying to switch places and do it again, like musical chairs.

And so I thought all this would conspire to make it easier. But now I wish Kolohe would come back from wherever he is, because I am uncertain where to begin about Japan, and he was a good excuse for not beginning.

Though so much has been written about Japan, the Japan that was in my mind before I went there was an unlikely amalgam of the Japanese Twins in Old Tokyo (the Twins series was big when I was growing up) and World War II, plus the vigorous vibes from a fairly new, small, sturdy Japanese car in our garage at home, a bright green Datsun that lives frugally and works hard. And now it isn't easy to isolate the bit that I really saw.

It was a year ago that I was there with my husband for a few weeks, doing most of the things tourists do. That should be long enough for the tea leaves to settle, so you'd think, into a clear picture in the bottom of the mind. Yet they stay in suspension. Or, worse, they melt creamily together as clouds do, leaving no line, an amorphous situation that is hard on writer and reader alike. It tends to breed footnotes, with every footnote, like a diligent hamster, breeding nine more.

Too, another language presents a recurrent and bothersome problem: Should the foreign word be used if there is no English synonym, and its translation be footnoted? Or not? Or, to put it another way, should the writer bore the reader who knows the word, or annoy the reader who doesn't?* Or, to drive the safe middle lane, should little Chiyoko exclaim, "Oh, Grandma, see my beautiful new white cotton bifurcated Japanese footgear [*tabi*]!"? . . .

I think I can only try my best to hold the footnotes to a minimum. Better still, I think I won't have any more. If I feel a footnote coming on, I will number it and put it among the Notes at the back of the book (for this chapter they begin on page 264).

—The mental memos and the sounds that stay in the head. "Yes, the window will not open, no?" And the maid in the hotel hallway singing about a rong rong trail awinding, as we headed for the bath, and how right she was. And the portly Santa Barbara blonde at the beauty shop, "Make me look like a geisha girl!" And the jungle noises of the subway, and somewhere the frail wail of the samisen, and the tea girl's snap of the red tea cloth.

And the practical matters. How do you put on a kimono? Well, you generally carry it in a big box to the corner hairdresser's; they will dress you in it properly for a thousand yen, and a good thing, too, or you would never make it to the temple on time. With all its moving parts, it is a complicated piece of work as well as—possibly—one reason Cho-Cho-San is such a faithful little thing, the kimono being about as hard to get out of as into.

(The kimono isn't to be confused with the *yukata,* by the

* " 'No mortal but is narrow enough to delight in educating others into counterparts of himself'. . . . The Anglo-Indian who has discovered that the suttee he read of as a boy is called *sati* by those who know it best is not content to keep so important a piece of knowledge to himself; he must have the rest of us call it *sati,* like the Hindoos (ah, no—Hindus) & himself; at any rate, he will give us the chance of mending our ignorant ways by printing nothing but *sati* & forcing us to guess what word known to us it may stand for."   —H. W. Fowler

way, or, more accurately, is often confused with the *yukata,* which is the crisp cotton robe awaiting the overnight guest in most Japanese hotels. It must be worn with the left front panel brought over the right front panel unless one is being buried in it, and its sleeves tend to drag the teacups around; otherwise, it makes an excellent bathrobe.)

But the first question leads inevitably to a second: Why should anyone put on a kimono in the first place? There is something so compliant about a kimono, something so humble and hobbling. (Chinese bound feet, Western bustles, stiletto heels.)

But why today? Aesthetically, the kimono's main advantage is that it hides bad legs, those short sturdy parentheses produced by centuries of kneeling. And many a Japanese girl has good legs today, at least better than her mother's. She's eaten more protein, sat on more chairs, while her mother grew up eating more rice than vegetables, more vegetables than fish, and kneeling, kneeling, kneeling. . . .

But what do I know about it? And who is to say what is a bad leg or a good leg? Short muscular bowlegs look good to the glistening Japanese eye, the way the nape of a woman's neck does. There is something tender, vulnerable, sensual about the feminine nape, and the exquisitely adjusted kimono shows just enough of it to have Papa-san breathing fast. And so there are kimonos aplenty among the minis.

There it is, one thing melding with another. I hadn't intended to talk about kimonos right there, or fast breathing, either. So I retreat to the scraps and tatters, the picture postcards of the mind.

There is the nice hot family bath we took in an inn in Nagoya, the stream modestly rising to obscure our bright pink nudity, my husband's and mine, as we simmered like artichokes, lacking only a touch of garlic to be perfectly delicious, and tried to think rarefied thoughts while cooking. "Bathing of the Japanese is far beyond the simple object of cleaning their body, but is so evolved that they take bath to wash their *life!*"—as Mr. Fujimoto put it so enthusiastically in our guidebook.

Right on, Mr. Fujimoto! My life was not only cleaner but shorter, I reflected a bit later, just before I passed out on the floor of the hall. *Always add cold water to your Japanese bath.* (In my own notes this one was underlined.)

And here is a memo on the back of a Shinto fortune slip. That was a real pleasure, I thought—much better than the morning astrology column back home—getting your daily nudge at the red Shinto shrine. Only twenty yen, and if you don't like it, tie it like a blossom to the tree, and leave it behind for the pretty Shinto priestesses to deal with. They trot about in their red skirts and white shirts, even dance at your wedding, if you're good to the shrine. I think the shrine likes sake[1]; fat straw-bound bales of it adorned the courtyard.

But Kolohe interrupted me there, leaping up again to rearrange my notes and remind me the sun was high and it was time to go snorkeling off the front yard.

Sometimes he paces the beach when people go in the ocean, but more often he sits and watches. From the tranquil water this side of the reef I can usually see him, motionless on a small arc of shore that looks nearly as Japanese as it does Hawaiian, the way the pagoda roofs curve black against the sky and the dark mountains loom beyond. It is the shiny palm fronds and lush color that reiterate Hawaii.

There he sits, small on the white sand, sitting at alert, looking very much like an ornamental plaster cat I bought from a stall in the Asakusa part of Tokyo to guard my office at home. I don't want to omit him, either, for he is quite a famous cat, this *manikeneko*. He is known as the beckoning cat, and he is eternally sitting, with his left front paw raised to his right ear, the pink pads showing (because that is the way the Japanese beckon—the palm of the hand toward you, with the fingers curled down).

It seems that the original live cat belonged to a famous geisha; and one day he started making a noisy nuisance of himself, meowing and clawing her kimono while she entertained a lover. Understandably annoyed, the lover finally whipped out his sword and cut off the cat's head, which immediately flew up to the rafter and killed a poisonous snake who was coiled there, ready to strike. This was a cat of great character, you see, faithful beyond death. He had only been trying to warn his mistress of the imminent danger.

Of course she felt terrible about it, legend continues, and she mourned and mourned. Legend doesn't mention what she did to her lover, though I imagine she fixed his little red ricksha. But at least she had a statue of the cat made, and replicas are everywhere now, as good-luck tokens or—inscrutably—as coin banks. Cat banks, not pig banks. The one I have is white plaster with dark-centered yellowed spots, like black-yolked fried eggs, and an orange nose and a red collar, a superb example of Japanese kitsch, though with his big solemn black eyes and alert ears he is still a very sincere-looking cat, like an earnest Boy Scout.

But I doubt if it is solicitude that has Kolohe watching me so patiently while I am in the water. I'm afraid it is appetite. He knows there are fish out there. He doesn't know I have no intention of acquiring one for him, even if I knew how. I only float, mindless and easy, like a bigger fish in a face mask, over the coral tenements in the sun-dappled water and watch the others—the rainbow fish and the globular black-striped yellow ones and the big translucent ones, the ghost-fish and the spirit fish, and the eels that slip, shadowlike, through the seaweed, and the hours slip away, too.

And so another day has gone by, and I'm no closer than I was to creating order out of this particular chaos, the Japan that is on my desk and in my mind. The little country that smells like green tea and exhaust fumes and incense and sewage. The formidable Land of the Risen Sun, the tough, delicate East-West land of the nuclear power plant and the bullet train, the group-think and the group-move, the giggle and the geisha, the yang and the yin, the gray-green gardens, the doves, the Seven Lucky Gods, and the huge department store the subway pours people into, like milk into a cup.

—A marvelous department store (Macy's, Gimbel's, Bloomingdale's, eat your hearts out!), and if the clerks had spoken English I would probably be there still, washing rice bowls in the sub-subbasement to earn passage home. Fortunately, I didn't know there were translators and guides. All I bought was a Camembert cheese (because one gets hungry for cheese in Japan) and a small mask of fat, beaming Ebisu (because he looked so appealing).

He is one of the Lucky Seven, and the elderly clerk who waited on me had to thumb his dictionary thoroughly in order to explain Ebisu's *raison d'être*. "He is to keep the mind smiling," he finally came up with, in some triumph, after trying numerous words for size.

> That's a great big job,
> To keep someone's mind smiling!
> Good old Ebisu!

Now, that was a haiku, more or less—those three lines. That is something else I keep running across in the confetti here—haiku. And perhaps they would be a good place to start, for I found haiku as contagious as they seem to find them in Japan, where haiku-writing is rather a nervous national habit. When the Japanese are not sipping tea or downing sake or building an immense factory or a microscopic computer, chances are good that they are writing a tiny haiku, though that is like saying two twins, for the haiku is tiny by definition, being a sort of seventeen-syllable[2] poetic hiccup (haikup) that usually sounds like a note for a poem somebody is going to write, someday. Having no rhyme or perceptible rhythm, the haiku isn't hard to do if you can count up to seventeen[3], which is one reason for its popularity with U.S. primary-school teachers, who have the moppets writing them by the wastebasketfuls. Another reason is neatness, for it certainly beats Creative Clay Play. Best of all, perhaps, it gives the children the good feeling that they have written a poem.

And so it is that I keep running across these little verse droppings about the Japanese,

> a nonfrivolous folk
> fond of bowing, stocking feet,
> and eating pickles

—though it is apparent from this one that I have a lot to learn about writing haiku or counting, one or the other. However hard I tried, I couldn't get rid of the extra syllable in the first line—dropping the *a* changed the meaning in some subtle fashion—and it all gave me a healthy new respect for the first graders.[4]

A graver fault is that the verse leaves so much uncovered, like those Japanese pickles, which certainly need covering, with something like a lead blanket, and then they should be left undisturbed. Unlike the haiku, the Japanese pickle is nonaddictive. You can quit, cold turkey, with virtually no withdrawal symptoms except relief.

For centuries, apparently, the Japanese have floundered

pathetically around in the pickle department, using all sorts of implausible things to make their pickles out of, like egg-plants and turnips and radishes; and with a stumble-footed start like that, it's no wonder they can't think of anything else to do but age or rot them in fermented bran paste.

Consequently, the Japanese pickle is to the all-American pickle as the anteater is to the bicycle, different species that couldn't possibly interbreed, and that is just as well. It's a shame that when we gave Japan all that technological assist-ance after the war we didn't include a good pickle recipe.

I am not the one to write about Japanese food[5], I know, because I haven't a proper appreciation of it.[6] Mainly, I found it too pretty to wear and not good enough to eat, and I kept thinking of the voice teacher who finally growled to his perspiring student, "I play on the white keys and I play on the black keys but you keep singing in the cracks." That is where they seem to cook.

Yet, in their defense, it must be remembered that Japanese taste buds have been underprivileged for centuries as a result of poverty and Zen. These two things together gave them some fairly funny ideas of what tastes good—a point that is clearly illustrated by an incident in the life of Senrikyu, the Zen Buddhist who invented the tea ceremony. I found an account of it, by Itsugai Kajiura, in a book I bought at a Tokyo bookstall.

One wintry day back in the sixteenth century, the shogun dropped in on Senrikyu for lunch. That was his first mistake. Surely he was aware that Senrikyu was a Zen cook; and the true Zen cook lives off the land, feeling at one with a mush-room when he meets a mushroom, at one with a turnip when he meets a turnip, and abiding at all times by three main principles: don't spend money when cooking, don't be luxu-rious, don't buy anything.[7]

Senrikyu didn't have much in the house, but he didn't let this rattle him. Excusing himself, he went out to the snowy garden and picked a *yuzu*. This is a member of the tangerine family and completely inedible, even to the Japanese.

But this didn't stump Senrikyu. He removed the fruit, stuffed the rind with bean paste, and broiled it. He also made soup out of some black beans, water, and a bit of sugar, and —as an afterthought—threw in a stale rice cake someone had given him, some weeks earlier, which had become too hard to bite.

Senrikyu thought the resulting lunch was pretty good, which I suppose isn't surprising. Any cook who manages to pull a last-minute rabbit out of a hat tends to overestimate it. But the big point here is that the shogun liked it, too; it was a smash. So, in any consideration of Japanese tastes, these things must be taken into account.

Perhaps my most illuminating encounter with real Japanese cooking was an inexplicable breakfast I had, in the course of which I only recognized the egg. (The hen is a true world citizen.) There is a note here on my desk about that breakfast, which Yumiko brought to our room at the inn one morning—a lovely fresh morning in Beppu, one of those mineral-bath resort places on the southern island of Kyushu.

Outside the window, puffs and curly plumes of white steam softened the roofscape, and cherry blossoms misted the black hills by the Inland Sea. (I feel that I must include these details to make it clear that the setting was one in which almost anything would have tasted good.)

Yumiko was a friendly desk clerk, round and smiling and studying English, and she did her level best to tell me what was in all those little nonmatching dishes.[8]

Together we worked our way through the breakfast soup

—the *misoshiru*—made of fermented soybean paste, fish stock, seaweed, and fried bean curd. (Yumiko said the girl who makes good *misoshiru* makes a good wife.) And the pickled seaweed, and the vegetables and fish mixed with bean curd and fried with ginseng root, and the soybean noodles. And the eggplant and radishes pickled in salt. (Yumiko said that the girl who is good at pickle-making is good at love-making. She was full of these one-liners.) And finally the dark green nori, seaweed with the taste of cod-liver oil and the texture of crisp carbon paper.

When I faltered, she prodded me gently, saying that every time you eat something new, your life will be prolonged by seventy-five days—an old chestnut they're much given to quoting over there, probably thought up by some Japanese mother to get Junior to eat his nice seaweed. But just in case there was something in it, I tried everything. Totaled up, I thought it might cancel the reverse effects of the hot Japanese bath we'd had the day before, which had rather melted my candle, at least at one end.

But now it is late in the afternoon, and I am unaccountably hungry. We are going to go out in the front yard to watch the sun set—it usually drops with considerable glory behind Molokai—and then go eat some pot roast at a teriyaki place. (Teriyaki is all right if you like maple syrup on your sirloin.) Then we will probably come back here and sit outside for a bit, watching the quiet ocean scallop the beach, and probably we'll listen in spite of ourselves to the old pineapple peddler go into his act next door.

The temple hires out the mission hall behind it on week nights, frequently to a hard-working Japanese-Hawaiian pineapple packer who public-relates The Pineapple to tourists he lures out of the big hotel lobbies with the promise of a ukulele band and free *mai tais*.[9]

Then, after his pineapple pitch, he teaches the blue-haired ladies to hula. ("Okay, girls! Swing it! Swing it to the *right,* now swing it to the *left!* I wantcha ta putcher—uh—*hearts* into it! C'mon, gang!") After all these weeks he has the script letter-perfect, and one night they played the *huki-lau*[10] song five times.

Kolohe and I have achieved a working agreement now, I think—I work, and he's agreeable, if I talk to him and rub his ears first thing, and give him a good breakfast before I start to type. Then he curls up on the bookcase and eyes me narrowly, wondering why I am doing this, I suppose, as I wonder, myself, unless it is to prove what I said some chapters ago about the incommunicability of traveling. I don't know how to pin down the chiffon feel of the air here, or how to work in it very long, either.

Cat and weather aside, there are other distractions. This morning I talked for a bit with the priest next door—Mr. Hara—as he did some weeding at the foot of the Buddha in the Jodo temple yard.

He is a tall, pleasant, close-cropped young Japanese, not long away from Japan; and he smiles and nods and bows a good deal, I think to compensate for his faulty English. He told me several things—that this was the biggest Buddha outside Japan, and explained, by the way, about the Buddha's ear lobes. I hadn't noticed, but they are usually pierced for earrings, he said, because, like most Hindu princes, Buddha wore them before he took up religion.

He also took me into the pagoda, where they keep the ashes of the faithful, a light, cheerful place. And naturally enough, for if death is only a necessary step for every living thing along the way to the inevitable attainment of Buddha-hood, as Mr. Hara says, it's certainly nothing to be dreary about.

Another interesting thing is the way the Jodo sect makes the picture still brighter. As Mr. Hara explained it, only a complex mind can really understand the complexities of the Buddhist doctrine. But Jodo teaches that simpler souls can make it to the Pure Land, too, if they will do the very best they can and frequently repeat the holy words *Namu Amida Butsu* (which means Let us worship the Buddha Amida).

It seemed like an excellent idea to me, broadening the membership base this way—eminently fair, and it would also make for more congenial company in the Pure Land when you eventually got there.

But this morning I want to write about our afternoon at Ichuru Kanbayashi's house in Kyoto. (It occurs to me only now that the house remains in my mind as his, not theirs, though his wife was there, too. But she tends to recede, as Japanese women have been trained to do.)

Mr. Kanbayashi, who immediately asked us to call him Jimmy, was an interpreter for a big ball-bearing company, a friend of a friend of a friend of ours in San Francisco. He had telephoned us that morning in Kyoto to say he understood that I had written some books and might like to see Japanese way of life at home.

I was delighted to have the chance, for according to my Japanese agent—a knowledgeable Arkansas traveler who married a Japanese and settled in Tokyo—they seldom invite you home unless you've one foot on the train step and they know you can't come.

Jimmy picked us up at our inn that cold rainy afternoon, put me in the back seat of his Toyota and my husband in front, then plunged intrepidly into the traffic and across town, to a street of shops and garages and brown frame houses with wet gray tile roofs spiky with TV aerials under a soaked rice-paper sky.

A short, round-shouldered, cheerful, somewhat intense man, he walked quickly, head down, hands behind his back, as he hurried us through the gate in a tall wood fence and across his scrubby yard—a very dry garden indeed, comprising weeds, dirt, two rocks, and a tricycle. (It is always a pleasure when a stereotype bites the dust—nice to meet a stolid blond Frenchman or a black with no rhythm—and it was refreshing to find a Japanese nongardener.)

On the top stair of the entrance to a dark anteroom, we left our shoes, long and Western beside the ones already there, and padded down a dark hall to a room where his wife waited with two friends.

Mrs. K. was a small neat woman in a gray sweater and skirt who looked thirty and was probably forty. Another, a quiet lady in a dark suit, taught English literature at the university, Jimmy explained, but read the language better than she spoke it. The third and youngest, Setsuko, was as glorious as a geisha—flowered silk kimono, snow-white *tabi*. She was a pretty girl with a degree in anthropology and a job in a dress shop, just like anywhere. She had worn kimono, she explained, because she thought I might be curious about all the trappings—the underthings and cords and sashes.[11] ("But how do you stay warm and dry outdoors on a day like this?" I asked her later on, as the rain rattled on the roof like gravel. At which the pretty little thing untied her *furoshiki*—the big versatile handkerchief that's a handbag, lunchbox, briefcase, whatever you like—and happily shook out a pink satin three-quarter coat, her *haori,* about as practical as a lace dishrag.)

This was a *kokuteru* house, Jimmy said, *kokuteru* meaning cocktail or mixture—part Eastern, part Western—and we were apparently in its Western hemisphere now.

It was a large room, big enough to accommodate some overstuffed chairs, an overstuffed sofa, and—oddly—twin beds, plus an upright piano, a roll-top desk, a fireplace, and a *kotatsu*, the only Oriental note I saw, besides the teacups.

A *kotatsu* is a kind of communal foot warmer, and it is rather a chummy feeling to sit around one, like dunking for apples in the same tub. It is a hole in the floor that holds a charcoal-burning fire—a special sort of smokeless charcoal. Over it is a wood frame, about the height and size of a coffee table, covered with a quilt that hangs down like a tablecloth to hide your feet.

It was a comfortably used room, undoubtedly the living center of the house, which didn't surprise me. Those classically austere Japanese rooms have always seemed to me better to look at than live in.

—Not that the classic Japanese room isn't practical. When a room is all-purpose, four can live for the space of one. And of course it is beautiful. Ours at the inn was a perfect study in *shibui*[12]—subtly perfect proportions, the light softened by the creamy rice paper, the good wood unpainted, the window adroitly placed to frame the shadow of a twisted fir branch—all that. And fresh, plump, springy tatami on the floor. (It is said that tatami and wife are best when new.)

But an overnight room for a traveler is one thing, and a house for a family is another. What becomes of the relentless accretions of family living? How does the magician's tiger disappear in the visible emptiness of the slatted wooden cage?

The answer is, of course, that it doesn't. Tiger or clutter, it's only whisked out of sight, one way or another, as we saw later when Jimmy showed us the Japanese part of the house. I wouldn't want to criticize another woman's housekeeping, but never look behind a shoji screen.

Mrs. Kanbayashi poured tea and passed little cold sausage tartlets and chocolates.

It appeared that the conversation was to be mainly question and answer. I was to feel free, Jimmy explained, to ask anything I wanted. And so they sat, waiting like docile, alert children, Jimmy teetering back on the rear legs of a straight chair against the cold fireplace, the rest of us sitting around the warm *kotatsu*.

Taken by surprise, I felt impelled to seem more profound than I am.

"What do you consider Japan's biggest problem?" I began.

"Oho!" Jimmy said. (It turned out that he prefaced most of his answers that way, as though you had turned up a real nugget that enabled him now to turn up another one.) He uncurled one finger from a closed fist. "One: population. It is almost one-to-one ratio but still too many people." He uncurled a second finger. "Two: the gap between very rich and very poor."

"It is about the same in our country," I said. A dumb remark. I should never try to paddle in waters like these.

"Oho! I don't think so," he said. "In your country, the poor man eats turkey soup. Even though Mr. Rockefeller owns the turkey ranch, they both eat turkey soup."

I could see the basic truth here, though his example seemed wrong. Mr. Rockefeller would more likely be eating turtle soup, I thought, followed by breast of veal and a low-cholesterol chocolate mousse—and even so, it depends on which Rockefeller you're talking about—while the poor man eats the hamburger and Hostess cupcakes he got with his food stamps. I started to say so, but Jimmy stopped me at the turtle soup. "Not in Japan," he said, wagging his head. "We feed turtle in Japan, turtle not feed us."

"You don't eat turtle meat?' I asked.

He frowned. "*Some* do," he said. "But turtle is very lucky." He explained that when fishermen catch a turtle, it is customary to put the turtle upside down on the sandy beach, give it a good slug of sake, then put it back in the water. I thought the turtle was very lucky, too. *And,* he said, people who *do* eat turtle never kill it themselves. That would be enormously bad luck. There are special families of turtle killers—do nothing but kill turtles, generation after generation. "So!" he said triumphantly. "Have good luck and eat turtle, too!"

It seemed to me rather a shifty solution, but I didn't pursue the subject, because Jimmy was already uncurling Number Three Finger.

"Three: education," he said, and explained that the country had suffered from adopting the more or less democratic American system of education after World War II—before that it had been the more aristocratic and exclusory German system—and this had lowered the quality.

"I know," I said,[13] and told him what an elderly Japanese artist had said to us the day before: that no one under the age of forty-five could do decent calligraphy now.

"Oho! True!" said Jimmy. "But we don't need calligraphy." He sounded impatient. "Physics we need. Biophysics. Aeronautics."

He went on about this, but he didn't have my total attention. Across from us, the ladies were periodically giggling. While I knew this was only good manners, still it seemed remotely possible that they were giggling at my husband and me, for in truth we were having a hard time adjusting to the *kotatsu.* My husband's legs are long, and mine are short. Sitting side by side on the sofa as we were, and stuck with the same *kotatsu,* we really had a problem. What was the right distance for me had my husband's knees bumping his chin. Eventually we reached a compromise—if I lay back like the lead man on a toboggan while he hunched forward like a fullback hiding a football, we could keep our feet warm. But working it out satisfactorily took considerable footsie-wootsie (*futusi-wutusi*), and I didn't think the arrangement would ever replace central heating.

As the afternoon wore on, it seemed that Jimmy wanted to talk about big things, like Mitsubishi, and I wanted to talk—or ask—about bigger things, like women. (Electric companies come and go, but women go on forever.)

In fact, I wanted to talk *to* the women, but this posed problems. When I asked a question, they lowered their eyes or giggled, or both, and looked to Jimmy for the answer, as he teetered there on his chair, a hearty small rooster of a man, apparently in complete control of the henhouse.

I know this was partly because of their inadequate English. But equally (I felt) it was an inbred conviction that conversation was a male prerogative—a conviction that Jimmy apparently shared. As a result, the conversational ball had a noticeably peculiar triple bounce. I would ask a woman a question, and Jimmy would reply, but not directly to me, to my husband. Tinker to Evers to Chance.

He wasn't accustomed to talking to women, I learned later, when I asked why married couples in Japan so seldom go out together in the evening.

"Oho! Because Japanese wife can't talk about anything!" he replied (to my husband). And he said he was astounded when he visited the United States to find that many wives could talk as well to a man as any hostess at a sake bar. (The three women looked amused at that, but none seemed offended.) But, he continued, because Japanese wives seldom get out, they don't learn how to be interesting. (No job till you've had some experience, no experience till you've had a job.)

"Are wives happy to stay home every evening while their husbands go out?" I asked, or words to that effect meaning Why do they hold still for it?

"Oho! Do you know what it costs to eat in a fine restaurant?" (To my husband, of course.) "In your money, one hundred sixty dollars for four people. Eighty dollars for two people."

My husband gave a faint yipe. He had been dropping more yen than he thought.

"Yes, but all the same—" I began.

"Japanese wife is brought up to be thrifty," Jimmy explained. "She wouldn't want to spend so much money. And she knows when she gets married this is how it will be. Her husband goes but—company pays for it."

His wife spoke up then, hesitantly, looking at Jimmy. "But sometime we go out," she said. "*Sushi,* at *sushi* shop. Sometime."

He shrugged impatiently. "Yes, maybe—something little, we go. *Sushi, donburi*[14] . . ."

On impulse, I asked the women what they considered the best years of a woman's life to be. They thought, and sneaked side glances at Jimmy, and looked embarrassed. Then Setsuko said, "School years," and Mrs. Kanbayashi agreed. The little quiet woman said hesitantly she thought they still lay ahead.

"Japanese wife very busy anyway," Jimmy said. "House, children, community things. Now tell me this: Did you notice our automatic doors?"

My husband said no, we hadn't especially. Jimmy seemed disappointed. He thought Japan probably had more automatic doors in stores and office buildings than any other country. And nearly five thousand golf courses now. And he asked if we had ridden the bullet train (we had) and climbed the Tokyo Tower (we hadn't). I told him we'd planned to the other day, but it would have been too smoggy to see anything.

He shrugged again, philosophically. "We are economic animals," he said. "You have a saying, to make omelet, break eggs." (He didn't exactly say omelet, but his *l*'s were better than most.)

And so the conversation caromed along, and the afternoon grew late. Outside, the sky was a luminous pearl-gray, heavy with impacted wet, but the rain had stopped for a little.

Jimmy asked if we would like to see the rest of the house, and we followed him obediently into the hall. Scurrying ahead, he hastily closed a door, which I thought was probably the door to the Great Convenience Place, the *benjo*. No one had asked me if I wanted to powder my nose, and from what I had been reading in the papers, I was glad it didn't need powdering.[15]

In the helter-skelter kitchen, which looked more like a George Price drawing than a Japanese print, Jimmy proudly showed us the electric rice cooker beside the two-burner stove. (Two burners are enough, he explained, if you don't especially want your food hot.) Then we came to the guest room—the classic Japanese tatami-matted room, bare except for a few cushions and the tokonoma.

I was glad to see the tokonoma—a little dusty but nonetheless there. I'd missed it in the sitting room, where the only decorative objects were a bust of Beethoven (the identical one, incidentally, that my music teacher had on her piano when I was a child, and it gave me the identical feeling of mild depression) and the television set, if it may be termed a decorative object.

In various places, I'd heard and read that the color TV had virtually replaced the *tokonoma* as the heart of the house, which was understandable. There is a certain sameness about a *tokonoma* and a *kakemono*[16]—you don't want to stare at a spray of pussy willows all night, or one poem, either.

And yet there seemed a certain sameness to Japanese television, too—mainly baseball and weather, sumo wrestling and samurai westerns, with pretty mama-sans beaming at a new electric can opener. And the tokonoma offers some advantages. Arranging one can be creative therapy for the housewife, as well as a means of marital communication— prettier than a kitchen bulletin board, and just as expressive. Every little twiglet has a meaning all its own, and it's a thickheaded husband who doesn't get the message when he walks in the door. I suppose a spray of cherry blossoms would say one thing, and a good-size rock would say another.

All things considered, if I had to choose between the two, I suppose I would choose television. Though, happily, there is no real need to choose; one can have both, leaving the *tokonoma,* as the Kanbayashis did, for the delectation of the guest. Jimmy translated the poem on the scroll for me. Something about a day is long but a lifetime is short, or it might have been the other way around; the brushwork was handsome.

As we said good-bye (and we were sorry to), Jimmy was still concerned with things we should see and do when we returned to Tokyo and before we left Japan.

His wife asked if we had been to tea ceremony, and I said no. I am not fond of ceremonies—I would avoid all weddings and funerals, including mine, if I could. And Jimmy apparently didn't think it worth bothering with. "Sit on your knees—ow!" He stooped comically and rubbed his shins.

But Setsuko of the flowered kimono unexpectedly disagreed. "*Rub* tea ceremony," she said, with great earnestness. She meant love. Mrs. Kanbayashi whispered that Setsuko was a tea mistress—had studied the art for a number of years.

That is how it happened that the day before we left Japan, I went to a tea ceremony, in Tokyo. Once my legs straightened out again, I was glad I had gone.

The place was a small teahouse on a side street not far from the Ginza. Or perhaps it was in the Ginza—it is hard for foreigners to tell exactly where that particular circus begins and ends.

But the tea garden had precise boundaries. It was a quiet island of its own, a world in miniature, though not the whole world, only some of the nicest parts of it, magically reduced —mountains to rocks, rivers to rivulets, and the stone bridge to garden-bench size, so that I felt by turns somehow small as Alice when she shrank, then big as Alice when she grew, as I followed the path that wound among the gnarled ancient pines no higher than my knees.

My guidebook said that "the teamaker and guests gather together for the tea ritual much as Westerners might when inviting intimates to a cocktail party." But I have reflected since that that is where the similarity ends, and it's hard to see why the guidebook writer ever brought the matter up.[17]

Inside the teahouse, the tea mistress welcomed me with grave sweetness. She was a Japanese girl in red-and-black kimono who knelt on the tatami with another guest, an older Japanese woman in gray kimono, in a room innocent of furnishings save the flowering branch in the tokonoma, and the teamaking essentials. A small bronze stove, a china water jug, a dipper, a tea caddy, a bowl . . .

The tea mistress bowed, and so did we, as she gave us

each a doll's plate of sweets, a cube of sturdy purple bean jelly and a pink sugar rosette. Then, bowing and kneeling and bowing again, she performed the old rites with grace and gravity, with the identical movements perfected centuries ago and practiced ever since.

—Tended the stove. Wiped the tea caddy. Snapped the red linen cloth with a somber flourish. Washed the elegant bamboo whisk. Measured the powder. The water. Whisked it to a pale green froth. Then, kneeling, poured and served the bitter green tea with gentle grace and total attention. And the discipline of inner stillness slowly spread, gathering to an entity almost tangible in that little room. Until at length she said, simply, "Finish." Meaning end. Probably her only English word.

It pricked the tranquil surface tension, though for a little while a thin Lucite coating remained as I made my way back to the world outside the garden. Then it shattered to bits, there in the Tokyo street manic with people, loud with horns and bikes, exuberant with Coke signs and sake bars and gas pumps and *takushi* cabs. (Tokyo pizza, they say, is polished rice sprinkled with little bits of foreign pedestrians.)

So I walked toward the Tokyo Tower through a furry yellow smog that didn't soundproof anything, only wrapped the noise the more securely about the ears, and knew I had been permanently charmed by this *kokuteru* country, the whole so much greater than the sum of its short people and tiny rice balls and giant businesses, where so many things curl back to the Eightfold Pathway, like little brooks home to the main stream, and so many more pour straight as a power line toward the ever grosser GNP. And thought, too, that I could live in it a hundred years without understanding it, and so, perhaps, could Jimmy, without knowing quite which country or century we were in or even—precisely— wanted to be in.

This is another quietly breathing morning here on Maui, before sunup; and I find that I'm feeling almost that way now—somewhat uncertain of time and place.

This is such a no-color hour, neither the cool aquarelle look of Japan nor the hot poster color of Hawaii. Only quiet shapes that could be either land, any year, with the Buddha rounded against the slowly brightening sky, and the mission steps broad and square.

A little while ago, I went outdoors to fetch the punctual breakfast papaya that usually waits under the tree, half hidden where it dropped, like an Easter egg in the wet grass. Then when I came back into the study, I put all my papers back in the file folder, the file folder back into the suitcase. Another two days here and it will be time to go home.

While I was doing that, I remembered something I heard my father say once (my father's grandfather came from Ireland, which is another island in another ocean). I think my father was quoting another sentimental Irishman in his cups when he said that it's nice to have a little country for your homeland, because it is easier to carry it in your heart. And I thought, Yes, and sometimes you discover that you have made room for two or three.

*Postscript*

It was while I was writing these last few pages in Hawaii that we noticed a great and unusual busyness next door—a great pounding and sawing and scrubbing and polishing going on over at the temple, with occasional harsh booming squawks, like Canada geese preparing for takeoff, as the temple maintenance men tested the PA system.

Then we realized that they were getting ready for a birthday party that the reverend Mr. Hara had mentioned to me —the Jodo sect's eight hundredth anniversary, to be celebrated there on the following Sunday. And as it turned out, it was a gala occasion for everyone, including even Kolohe, that cat of so many important affairs and responsibilities.

From Japan came the fragile old chief abbot of the order, Shinko Kishi. They carried him over the green grass in solemn procession that day, grand in his stiff purple robes and homemade wooden palanquin, up the steps and into the temple, followed by all the Japanese and Filipinos and Chinese and Hawaiians and mainlanders who had assembled there this sunny morning.

The venerable abbot stepped forward then, small and bald under his odd boat-shaped hat, looking like an ivory netsuke carved with faithful attention to detail, the man himself nearly lost in the heavy ceremonial gear.

"I am eighty-four years old and I have come here with the preparedness that this will be my final farewell to you," he said gently. His eyes were dark and tired, and his voice was reedy. It was clear that he had oceans still to cross, and miles to go.

And so he spoke for a few minutes, only a short speech, before he blessed the congregation. Then, before the Buddha and the golden lanterns and the lotus, the priests and bishops together chanted the sutras till the room rang with a fine round resonance, like a great bronze bell.

Lunch, a little later, was a cheerful picnic in the mission hall, open on three sides to the blossomy trade winds. Japanese *sushi,* deep-fat-fried bean curd, Korean *kimchi,* Hawaiian poi, Yankee hot dogs, and—to honor the important visitors—a trio of little girls in fresh-picked ti-leaf skirts and plumeria *leis,* who came to dance a hula on the grass.

Their ritual *aloha* kisses remained rosily on the abbot's old cheek and left him looking rakish but delighted. Then the girls danced to a somewhat scratchy phonograph record, the two smaller ones keeping a careful eye on the slightly older girl in the middle. (Watch the hands. If you are a little end girl in a hula line and the big middle girl is doing a sunrise beyond the reef, you'd better be doing the same thing.)

That was the moment Kolohe chose to stroll toward us across the yard, his tail high and waving, to investigate these odd goings-on at closer range and to tangle, perilously, with the agile brown feet of the busy little girls.

Disaster loomed, till the abbot suddenly reached far forward to swoop Kolohe up in his arms and cradle him there, gently and absently stroking the little cat for the rest of the program as the vivid children danced in the sunshine.

The abbot's face was serene, and I think that Kolohe's mind was smiling. I know that mine was, too.

# 17

---

## Last Chapter

*Which is only an epilog*

Arriving the other day at the heliport near San Francisco, I stayed a moment after I got off the helicopter to watch it take off again. It was a sturdy little chopper, noisy and windy but friendly, and I liked the way it left. No nonsense about it—just rose and departed, the way a good guest should at the end of a party, or an author at the end of a book.

That's the way to go, all right, and I made up my mind to do it—a decision made easier by discovering midway through the final chapter that it was about to become another book in itself, one that I didn't have the many-leveled knowledge to write.

This final chapter was going to be concerned with some of the real wonders of the world, the ones people really remember and marvel over, not the ones bearing the Good Travelers' Seal of Approval that make the official lists. I had asked a great many friends and acquaintances about this in the course of the past year, without realizing quite how personal a question it is, or how hard to answer.

Nor had I realized how hard it would be to find a pattern in all the answers. For here I am with a sheaf thick enough to thatch a roof—a list of wonders that includes the sunset from the top of the Jungfrau, and the Stones of Clava; the world-gone-away stillness of an Iowa wheatfield, and Picasso's *Guernica;* the moment of the moonshot, and the taste of a Romanée-Conti '64; and the first landfall, and the first baby, and several hundreds of other things.

And the list continues to grow. Yesterday at the doctor's office, I asked my question of the receptionist. She thought a moment and said, "Well . . . first . . . my father." (Who can argue with that?) And when I asked Tom Stone, fisherman and physician, about the wonders he had seen, he mentioned the unbroken immensity of sea and sky in the Mexican waters where he fishes, but said he had seen nothing yet to equal the human body, with its "intrepid and imaginative ways of renewing itself." And another man I know brought the focus down still finer to the opposable thumb.

My only sure conclusions are that wonder lies in the eye of the observer, and that a list like this, as Auden said of a poem, is never finished, only abandoned.

Now I remember back to the woman with the gray topknot some miles and chapters ago, sitting beside me on the plane home from Mexico City, and her husband, who met her—the man with the brown cardigan and the homemade greenhouse—and I wonder how the wildflowers are doing. There are many trips, and many ways to travel, and many a wonder, sure enough. It would be hard to say truly who had seen the most.

*When you've seen 145,000 mountain peaks you've seen 'em all.* —MONTANA TOURIST

# Notes

CHAPTER 1

A nice sense of when to speak, if ever, to the person beside one is a good part of airplane manners, or jetiquette. Anyone reading, writing, or sleeping probably wants it that way —would rather read, write, or sleep than talk. But if he is reading and you feel talkative and what he is reading looks dull, you can tell yourself that perhaps he is finding it dull, too, but he is shy. In this case, it is proper to proffer a tentative "Gamorning" or "Dafternoon" or "Devening," whichever you think it is after all those time zones. Now he has two choices: he can acknowledge with a simple nod that it is, indeed, whichever you said it was, or he can pick it up with enthusiasm and carry the ball forward.

\* It is rather impolite as well as unwise to take off your shoes in an airplane unless you've brought slippers or airplane socks along. Feet often swell up, as a result of Boyle's Law (page 262), so you can't get your shoes on again right away; and it can be awkward to stocking-foot it down the ramp.

\* People who need to go to the bathroom frequently or like to stretch out their legs and admire their new shoes or enjoy walking around a great deal in the airplane should choose aisle seats.

CHAPTER 3

One of the important functions of the comprehensive travel guide (page 26) is to forewarn the traveler about the times when things happen and don't happen—about the peculiar OPEN and CLOSED hours of museums, sights, shops, bars, grocery stores, and so on. And about festivals, saints' days and other holidays, which generally scramble things so that what you came to see is precisely what you cannot see. One of the functions of the traveler is to read these forewarnings, too, though he often doesn't, because they are generally buried in a thicket of fine print.

Museums usually operate with a certain contrariness—open when you'd like to picnic in the woods, and close when you'd like to look at pictures, especially if you are leaving the next morning. Whichever museums loom large on the itinerary should be carefully checked out. (Though the Matisse Chapel in Vence, for instance, is open only four and a half hours a week, it is worth planning a trip around —even worth the price of the overseas air fare, at least one way.)

And pub laws can be disconcerting, if your personal tippling hours don't match the government's. It is good to know that ahead and prepare for it.

And stores, of course—the French department stores that close on Monday, the provincial stores, every kind, that stop for lunch every day, the Dutch shops that close Monday mornings, and so on, and on . . .

\* Matters of time and timing are equally the concern of a good travel agent. Besides getting you to places at a time when you've a reasonable chance of seeing them, a travel agent who isn't merely a tour peddler will help plan a trip so that you come to an occasional restful halt in the surroundings you enjoy the most (so a beach nut doesn't spend a four-day layover in the heart of London, or a theater buff take his R&R on the beach).

About travel agents, by the way: it is important to have

one, because his services cost you nothing or next to nothing; and these days, doing your own complicated trip—like your own brain surgery—will nearly always result in a mussier, more expensive, and more painful, experience than you had planned on.

The best kind of travel agent has curiosity, unquenchable enthusiasm, and a good memory; and he has traveled to Hellengone and back many times. The first question to ask a new one is "When were you there last?" (Though you shouldn't have a new one very often; it should be a continuing affair.)

It is helpful, I think, to know how he gets paid. Because his fee is buried in the cost of the merchandise, the travel agent is delicately poised between mammon and conscience, as so many people are. He gets a rebate from certain things like airlines, European railroads, and large de-luxe hotels, like Hilton and Inter-Continental and Sheraton. But he receives none from American railroads, Canadian railroads, buses, and most other hotels, which are full to bursting anyway. (Does a popular girl need a date bureau?)

Therefore, the travel agent tends to think of the more lucrative carriers and hotels first, in planning your itinerary. And the more offbeat and personal the trip is, the more probably he'll need to charge a moderate service fee. (A bargain round-trip flight for a twenty-one-day European trip is, say, $354. The travel agent gets 7 per cent of that, or $24.78. If he makes eighteen out-of-the-way hotel reservations, at a minimum office cost of two dollars per letter, he must make it up with a service fee or go in the hole (though if he thinks the customer will be arranging other trips with him, he may not, on the principle of lose it on the apples, make it up on the bananas.)

Most travel agents don't mind explaining what they are paid for and what they aren't; and the traveler should ask, if he is in doubt. The traveler, too, is delicately poised between wanting plenty of tender attention—after all, this trip is important to him—and not wanting to be considered a total pain in the neck.

CHAPTER 4

Like film critics, the guidebooks don't always see eye to eye. Concerning Simpson's-in-the-Strand, the famous old roast-beef house in London, favorite of Sherlock Holmes and Dr. Watson:

Fodor's *Europe 1971:* "Stronghold of first-class meat (you must tip the carver 1 shilling per person and basically British. The vegetables have been known to disappoint, but the beef and lamb are superb."

*Holiday Magazine Guide to London,* 1972: "Simpson's is universally acknowledged to pass the highest standards in a field in which English claims to supremacy have never been disputed: to wit, the preparation of roasts and joints. The beef and mutton here are fantastic."

*Fielding's Travel Guide to Europe,* 1972: "Simpson's . . . currently evokes the image that it is riding a bit too hard on its long and distinguished reputation. It pains us deeply to state this, but we feel that it's slipping. Men's Bar in cellar and venerable, paneled, ground-floor restaurant (ladies admitted to latter only Sats.); rich, decorous, comfortable main restaurant up 1 flight (ladies always welcome). Our latest lunch was a jolting disappointment. The traditional timidity of the average Yankee in London Towne, coupled with the notion that 'If we find it at Simpson's, it *must be* how the British do it best!', possibly have conspired to allow this house to reign on as a venerable institution."

Frommer's *Europe on $5 & $10 a Day,* 1972–73: "Simpson's . . . a world-famous, and yet relatively inexpensive, restaurant which concentrates on the few food specialties that the English do well . . . tradition requires that you tip the carver separately (at least 5 pence). . . . This, I repeat, is a required stop for at least one lunch or dinner; your trip to London will be incomplete without it."

And my own notes about the place, the first time I ate there, don't really clarify anything: "Simpson's-in-the-Strand: chaste green walls, no wonder called the ladies' room. Aylesbury duck and applesauce recommended by nice Irish waiter, Mr. Beston, 4 kids and yearns to go to America. Pointed out Egyptian lady dining alone, ṣhot husband dead. Fahinia Bey, sounds like Turk. naval base, pretty lady tho. Duck good. Mr. B. also said headwaiter takes majority of tips, which are put in the *tronc,* then divided, so one leaves something sep. for waiter."

Rereading my notes, I wonder why Mr. Beston was pushing the Aylesbury duck instead of the beef. Perhaps the kitchen overbought and the waiters got a bounty per order. Anyway, he showed a nice knack for taking care of himself, and if he ever made it to the U.S. he is probably a corporation president now.

It is clear that it depends on whom you read. Fodor clearly didn't care for the Brussels sprouts; *Holiday*'s sweeping generalization doesn't stand up under close analysis; Fielding strikes a note of paternal reproof, a kind of this hurts me more than it'll hurt you; and Frommer seems to me to be wildly optimistic about that five-pence tip. Even though five British pence equal twelve of ours now, I have a feeling that any American who tips five pence anywhere is going to get them back, one at a time, right in the eye.

### Some Other Ways to Meet People
A traveler can ask his travel agent or the country's national tourist board or embassy about its meet-the-people project,

if it has one, as so many places do—Paris, Denmark, Italy, Sweden, Finland, Amsterdam, Jamaica, and a number of others. Or he can ask the national tourist board if they can help meet someone specializing in his own specialty, as they usually can.

In England, he can try the Private Home Program (be met at the station, wined and dined, bedded and breakfasted, at a reasonable rate). The address is The Old Orchard, Long Compton, Shipston-on-Stour, Warwickshire, England.

Or ask anyone at all at home, including the dry-cleaner's clerk and the delicatessen man, if they have relatives or old friends to whom he can bring personal greetings.

Or take a lesson or two when he arrives—skiing or skating or language or cooking or hula or flamenco or rapids-shooting or tennis or golf, in any likely place.

Or he can go to a foreign meeting of any club he belongs to that has foreign affiliates.

Or make a pleasant deductible visit to the foreign branch of any international-type company he works for or ever did work for.

Or write a fan letter to someone whose work he admires, suggesting lunch or dinner. Writers and painters sometimes melt at the thought of a free meal, especially if their admirers know what they wrote or painted, and spell it right.

*It is ridiculous to say that individuals can go touring the world, get jolly with strangers and thereby head off government conflagration. But it just might help a little.* —HUGH MOFFETT

### CHAPTER 5

Some people do their note-making in the form of letters to someone, usually Mother, for who else would care? Then she keeps them, tidily bound with ribbon or an old extension cord.

But much depends upon Mother. Some mothers would be as bored as anyone else by all this unasked-for information. It is polite to explain that they needn't read it if they don't want to, just keep it. And still another problem can arise, one that isn't so easily solved, or so I find it. The possibility that someone else may read them rather muddies my notes; I find that I am putting down what I think would impress or amuse them, not what interests me, and the result is usually a bit long on sensitive perceptions.

\* Every photographer should bring a long-sleeved pull-over sweater with him, to use as an emergency darkroom for changing film outdoors. Take off the sweater; put your hands (with camera in one and film in the other) into the cuff-ends of the sleeves, pushing forward till they are in the dark roomy abdomen of the sweater, everything protected from the light. Then remove the exposed film and wrap it snugly, by touch, and put the new film in, ditto. Lots of luck.

### CHAPTER 8
*Some Good Things to Know About Lodgings*
It is highly advisable to put your hotel's name, address, and phone number in your wallet before leaving your hotel for the first time, in case you forget where you are. This is especially important in Oriental countries (because you probably can't pronounce where you are even if you know), though it is a wise precaution everywhere. If this is Tuesday it ought to be Belgrade, but there is always the off-chance it is Prague.

\* It is always a good idea to check a hotel bill carefully before checking out, especially the beautiful, perfect-looking, computer-type bill. Certain crafty places rely on the bill's authoritative cybernetic look to lull the guest.

But examine the other kind, too, to see what each charge is for. I heard about the word *clef* appearing on someone's bill, with a charge of twenty-five francs—about five dollars —hand scrawled and buried in a list of taxes. When asked, the cashier said it was for the room key; the guest hadn't handed it in yet. Chances are breathtakingly good that if he had already returned it without noticing the item, no rebate would have been made.

\* Big foreign hotels will hold your mail for you even though you're not staying there. Tell your friends to mark the envelopes HOLD FOR ARRIVAL, with the approximate date you'll be in the city. This way you can avoid the long American Express mail line. Ask the concierge to look in the "hold" mail under all your names—first, middle, and last—because there is no knowing under which one they filed your letters. Then tip him the equivalent of half a dollar.

\* If you're taking a cab in another country or currency, ask the hotel concierge what is a fair price from here to there, or have him ask the cabdriver, then tell you. This can obviate a small war at the end of the line.

### Cutting Hotel Expenses and Other Tips

The easiest way in most countries other than the U.S. is to engage a room without a bathroom. The bath and toilet down the hall are nearly always clean, and you meet more people that way. (A caftan or muumuu makes a good night-gown-and-robe and you can also wear it out to dinner.)

A good way to cut hotel expenses in the U.S. is to avoid the coffee shop for breakfast and room service for anything. Cookies, dried fruit, instant coffee, and an immersion heater all travel well in your suitcase. So do wine or whisky when properly swaddled.

In hotel talk, American Plan means all meals included,

so named because you never find this plan in America. (It used to be the rule back when the old Colonial inns were really private houses, and the traveler ate with the proprietor and his family.)

Modified American Plan, or MAP, means the price includes breakfast and dinner.

European Plan means you may eat in the hotel or elsewhere and will be charged accordingly.

B&B means Bed and Breakfast, or Brandy and Benedictine, depending on where you find it.

The GO plan means Guest Option. As operated by some of the resort hotels in the Hilton chain, this means you pay a flat fee for a week, which covers room, airport-to-hotel-to airport transportation, and some little treat, like a cocktail party. It also leaves a slush fund that is applied to your other expenses—meals, hairdresser, bar, valet service, and so on.

If the place isn't brimful, most hotel managers will let you keep your room an hour or two after check-out time without charge, if you ask when you check in.

\* It is best to bring a cosmetic or shaving kit that can hang from its handle. Some bathrooms have no place but the floor to set anything down, but most doors have knobs.

\* If you need a place to type or write more comfortably in a hotel room, you can make a fair desk out of a coffee table (if it has a coffee table). Put a bed pillow on it, and on the pillow put an upside-down dresser drawer.

\* You never have to rummage and panic a little, at least about a hotel-room key, if you elect one standard place for it so it becomes automatic: say, the shelf over the washbowl, or the right-hand dresser drawer.

\* A rolled-up blanket or a big bath towel can lend authority to a puny bed pillow. So can the inflatable camp pillow.

\* A plump cake of soap isn't hard to pack along and works better than the standard butter-chip size.

\* If you've finished the Gideon Bible or already know the ending, the telephone book can be uncommonly interesting. It tells you what to do in case of monsoons or tidal waves, and the yellow section indicates where the town's heart lies. Also in large cities you can look up famous people. It is always in some way refreshing to find that many of them actually have telephone numbers, just like anyone.

*Myself, I like to write a note as from a blackmailer, a lecher, or a spy, and blot it wet on the blotter, to pique my successor in the room.* —J. BRYAN III

*If you've never spent the night in a real hole, the place to do it is Mamatat, Tunisia. The residents live in hundreds of enormous holes as deep as twenty-five feet and the city hotel is constructed the same way, with several underground rooms and beds made of dried mud.* —GEORGIA HESSE

CHAPTER 9

The small essential things should be packed in the flight bag, pocket, or handbag that stays with you everywhere. For most people, this includes toothbrush and toothpaste and make-up or razor, as well as that one highly individual item, the insulin or the licorice or somebody's snapshot.

*Some Good Paper Items to Bring*
Some gift paper, folded flat.

Business cards or informal cards engraved or imprinted with name or name and address.

Strong brown Manila envelopes for mailing back menus or folders or whatever you can't quite bear to throw away.

Empty white envelopes for tips or thank-you notes or keeping sales receipts together.

Your address book.

And postage. Bring stamps from home, on domestic trips, so you won't need to disturb the hotel clerk's reverie or patronize the one-arm bandits that pass for stamp machines. For foreign trips, don't bother to bring any of the ready-stamped government-issue Aerograms available here, a reminder that sounds foolish. But I know a fond mother who sent her son in Europe half a dozen of these, all pread-dressed to her, to save him the money and trouble.

Some documentary proof that you own any foreign-made equipment or jewelry you're taking out of the country. Otherwise you might have to pay duty when you bring them back in. If you've had them for years or don't have the sales receipts, it is worth a trip to the local customs house or to the airport to have them registered. Find out just where, and allow plenty of time.

Shirt-sleeves. *When you have occasion to tuck up your shirt-sleeves, recollect that the way of doing so is, not to begin by turning the cuffs inside out, but outside in—the sleeves must be rolled up inwards, toward the arm, and not the reverse way. In one case, the sleeves will remain tucked up for hours without being touched; in the other, they become loose every five minutes.* —FRANCIS GALTON*

* Francis Galton, *Art of Travel or, Shifts and Contrivances Available in Wild Countries 1872* (Harrisburg, Pa.: Stackpole Books, 1971).

Socks. *The hotter the ground on which you have to walk, the thicker should be your socks. These should be of woollen, wherever you expect to have much walking; and plenty of them will be required.*

—IBID.

Dressing Gown. *Persons who travel, even with the smallest quantity of luggage, would do wisely to take a thick dressing-gown. It is a relief to put it on in the evening, and is a warm extra dress for sleeping in. It is eminently useful, comfortable, and durable.*

—IBID.

## CHAPTER 10

There are two other things the traveler can do about jet lag. Before a long air trip, he can quit smoking. Then he won't feel the jet lag so much as the need of a cigarette. This is an advantage all smokers have over nonsmokers: they always know they'll feel better when they stop smoking, almost as good as when they stop not smoking.

Also, the traveler can choose an unpopular flight, so he can remove the armrests, if they're removable, and lie down across three seats, with an eye mask along for sleeping in the daylight. A big safety pin is good to bring, too, in case the airplane curtains are the kind that need pinning together.

* If you have trouble with what you ate, it is wise to move to the right-hand side of the plane, if you are not there already. The reason is that when the pilot circles, in holding patterns, he usually makes left turns, which you don't feel

so much on the right. You can also ask for an icebag and lie back with it under your neck, shut your eyes, and try not to think about the dinner.

\* By the way, it isn't what you ate that makes you swell up in the air. You couldn't have eaten that much of it. It is because of Boyle's Law, passed in the seventeenth century, which says that the volume and pressure of a gas at constant temperature vary inversely, whatever that means. But what it means to the passenger is that the stomach expands when it is over five thousand feet in the air, so that the skirt or the pants are probably too tight. Wear something expandable, or unbutton a couple of buttons.

\* You should exercise on a plane just as much as you can, the doctors say, by walking around. This not only keeps other people awake and exercised, too, as you squeeze past, it keeps your own vital juices moving. But you get exercise on the big planes anyway, your seat being two blocks from the bathroom. I don't know what the doctors are worrying about.

For unknown reasons, people go to the bathroom oftener on 747's and DC-10's, by the way, than they do on smaller planes. Science is looking into this. Meanwhile, more people stay waked up and exercised and in the bathroom when you want to get in yourself.

\* There is also the matter of ears. When someone holds his nose, shuts his mouth, and blows, he is not necessarily expressing his opinion of the in-flight movie, he may be just relieving pressure on his eardrums. It often helps.

### How to Make Money Off an Airline
If you are promoted to first class because they oversold the flight (or for any other reason not of your own devising),

they cannot charge you for it, even for the brandy. That is a clear gain.

Conversely, if they bump you in the other direction, from first class downward, they owe you the difference in money, and a nice apology, too.

It is wise to snap to attention when they ticket your bag, and to have in your head the code letters of your destination airport. Sometimes a check-in clerk, in a momentary lapse, will ticket a bag with PDX or JFK when he means LAX, which in turn means that your bag will arrive considerably later than you do.

But if they lose your bag—really lose it, not merely misplace it temporarily—they must pay you three hundred fifty dollars if you went coach, or five hundred if you went first class. They assume, you see, that first-class passengers have costlier raiment in their suitcases than coach passengers do, though it is often the other way around because the first-class passengers spent so much money on their tickets.

Either way it isn't too bad. If you were en route to a protest march or a dogfight, you will probably come out ahead. Be sure to collect. (On the other hand, if you are bringing your suit of lights with ermine tails to the shah's birthday party, it is best to buy an additional personal-possessions policy before you leave. You would want this in case of theft, anyway.)

If you are fortunate enough to be bumped off your flight altogether and arrive more than four hours later* on the alternate flight they give you than you would have on the original one, they owe you the price of your air fare (minimum twenty-five dollars, maximum two hundred) in addition to your ticket refund if you have to cancel your trip. That is what the Civil Aeronautics Board says, and it could be a welcome piece of change. Remember to collect it.

---

* For an overseas flight. For a domestic flight it is two hours.

On the other hand, airport life-insurance policies aren't real money-makers for anyone except the life-insurance companies. People buy them mainly during bomb and hijacking scares. Otherwise, chances of winning the bet are so small that it is a poor gamble. Steady policy purchasers usually can't pass a slot machine or a gum-ball machine, either.

If you buy one, be sure you mail it to the beneficiary before you board the plane. Some people don't, either because they don't know any better or they don't want to get his hopes up. But if it is found on you after the plane drops, it doesn't count. That's the way life-insurance companies are.

One other point: when an airline postpones a flight for personal reasons—say, they can't find the captain, or the engine—you have a perfect right to switch to a competitor's flight, if there is one with an empty seat. As there probably is, if you make up your mind quickly. (Most people shilly and shally and shuffle their feet and confer with each other till all the other flights are filled, too.)

But if bad weather postponed the original flight, the other flights will probably be just as late. So it is best then to buy another paperback, if need be, and find a comfortable place to sit, remembering always that departing flights are not generally announced over the PA system in the cocktail lounge.

*The tableland of sanity upon which most of us dwell is small in area, with unfenced precipices on every side, over any of which we may fall.*

——FRANCIS GALTON

## CHAPTER 16

1. Sake is the 15 per cent alcohol rice wine that is the standard Japanese tipple. The better the rice, the better the

sake, though it's hard to tell how good it is, because it has been served hot ever since they discovered that heat makes an inferior brew taste better, as well as adding more socko to the sake. Mrs. Kanbayashi told me it also softens rough skin: add some to the bathwater. But this may be only the manufacturer's idea of a good way to use it up, just as Procter & Gamble like you to carve figurines out of soap.

2. Books on poetry technique make quite a point of those seventeen syllables—five in the first line, seven in the second, five again in the last. Then in some frail folio of Japanese verse you find something like this, by the famous Japanese poet Bashô:

> Matsushima!
> Ah, Matsushima, ah!
> Matsushima, ah!

The syllable count here used to baffle me—the poem still does—because on my abacus it comes to fifteen. Then I realized that that's because it is a translation from the Japanese. It probably had the right number, once upon a time, till the translator got hold of it. Properly, it should have been rendered more like:

> Matsushima, ah!
> Ah, Matsushima, aha!
> Ah, Matsushima!

To my mind this is an improvement, adding as it does a note of lyric discovery, as well as the required additional two syllables.

3. The Japanese start counting with their fists closed raising one finger per number. If they go on to twenty, they close their fingers again, one by one, and thus they needn't take off their *tabi*.

—————

4. The only thing to do in a situation like this, I eventually learned, is make a tanka (or waka) out of it. The tanka (or waka) gives you a comparatively lavish thirty-one syllables to work with—five, seven, five, seven, seven—and the poem could then read like this:

> Nonfrivolous folk,
> fond of bowing, stocking feet,
> and eating pickles,
> they go blossom-viewing now
> on jazzy souped-up Hondas.

But the Japanese are historically a frugal folk, as well as basically fondest of small things—diminutive trees, baby fish, tiny tidbits. If offered a choice between a meatball and a hamburger, they will take the meatball. Consequently, the tanka (hamburger) has never become as popular as the haiku (meatball) and is used mainly in emergencies.

5. Unless it's plain cooking like their French-fried shrimp or barbecued chicken, or a nice East-West blend, like *mizu-taki* or *sukiyaki,* which, like a Eurasian girl, can be absolutely luscious. Otherwise, the more Japanese it becomes, or remains, the more regrettable.

6. I felt better about this when Jimmy Kanbayashi told me that the Japanese male's dream is to have a Japanese wife, a French mistress, an English town house, and a Chinese cook.

7. Actually, this isn't too different from my grandmother's principle of make do or do without. She was a Kansas Presbyterian minister's wife, and I'd like to have a nickel for every time I've heard her say that. But she applied it mainly

to patching pants and so on, not to cooking. Though she could stretch a leftover a country mile, and grew her own vegetables, she bought her staples, and sometimes a parishioner would crash through with a barrel of apples. I don't think she ever felt at one with the apples, exactly, but she was awfully glad to get them.

8. To the Japanese, a Western plateful of meat, potatoes, and a vegetable is about as appealing as a dog's dinner. They consider the essence or emotion of each food—its *kimochi*—then serve it in the dish that best expresses it: high glaze, low glaze, brown, green, square, scalloped, round, fish-shaped, shell-shaped, whatever, and hardly anything matches anything else. And certain things are for certain things. Never serve anything but tea in a teacup, though I thought some of their teacups would be perfect for chocolate pudding.

9. The *mai tai* is a popular tourist drink. Properly made with assorted rums and good raw Hawaiian whisky, it is the prototype of the Missionary's Downfall. But usually it contains more fruit than alcohol, particularly if mixed by a pineapple man.

10. A *hukilau* is a sort of Hawaiian fish picnic—everyone lends a hand to pull in the netful of fish and then they cook it. They sing about it oftener than they do it.

11. Three separate cords tie down three separate pieces of underwear. Then comes the wide stiff ribbon called a *date-maki* and eventually, the thirteen-foot-long obi. It takes another three cords plus a great deal of honorable know-how to arrange the obi properly, so it will hold the cardboard in

the front and the pillow in the back. Apparently they never thought of tying the pillow in back low enough to sit on, which would have saved much wear and tear on the knees, over the centuries.

Mrs. Kanbayashi volunteered that though her family had been in the obi business for three hundred years, she wore kimono rarely—only for highly ceremonial occasions—and her husband made a little joke. "To Japanese wife, many strings attached," he said, and we all laughed heartily. It was a better joke than my husband or I could have made in Japanese, all right.

12. "*Shibui* means beauty that is understated, never obvious, deceptively simple while really being complex. The *shibui* object never proclaims itself—in color or line or material. It must wait for its depths to be discovered. This value applies to almost everything in Japanese life: architecture, gardens, foods, clothing, ceramic and lacquer ware, straw goods, etc. Even manners! In short, *shibui* is the main, most-sought-after value in Japanese esthetic life."

—ELIZABETH GORDON

My orange-red-white-and-black *manikeneko* cat is the exact opposite of *shibui,* but he is still a very fine cat.

13. It occurs to me that my husband was presumably sitting tongue-tied through all this, though of course he wasn't. I can't always remember who said what, and it's just easier to do it this way.

14. *Donburi* is an inexpensive meal in a bowl, an eel meal if eels are plentiful, or a chicken meal if chickens are, always with rice and usually with some *shoyu* sauce, the Japanese soy sauce. This is made from fermented soybeans, which should come as no surprise.

---

15. In spite of five thousand golf courses and the bullet trains, the old-fashioned *benjo* that most houses have is a far forlorn cry even from the oblong trough set flush in the floor that serves most public places, as I found once to my dismay in a suburban lunchroom. It is a big clay pot, generally ready to overflow and often effervescent with little live things. Too often the honey wagon cometh not on the days it is supposed to—not enough wagons or personnel, according to the paper. It's no wonder the Japanese don't want the toilet in the same room with the bathtub. I don't think I'd want it in the same county.

16. The *tokonoma* is an alcove containing a flower arrangement and the *kakemono,* a scroll or wall hanging generally involving some calligraphy. I found the two words easy to confuse till I wrote an unforgettable haiku:

> a tokonoma
> could hold a kakemono
> but not vice versa

It would have to be a large *tokonoma* to do this, of course, and you generally find the *kakemono* hanging to one side.

17. The tea ceremony is hard on the knees; the cocktail ceremony hard on the ears and the liver. Before honorable tea, one eats little sweet things; with honorable cocktails, little salt things. The tea ceremony gently underscores the four basic Zen virtues—harmony, respect, purity, tranquillity; the cocktail ceremony doesn't, exactly. And what is purposive with one is only a by-product of the other. Crawling through the low teahouse entrance fosters humility, but with the cocktail ceremony the humility sets in the next morning.